Best Wall Quilts

from McCall's QUILTING

Easy Patterns for Year-Round Decorating

Martingale
Create with Confidence

Best Wall Quilts from *McCall's Quilting:*
Easy Patterns for Year-Round Decorating
© 2012 by Editors of *McCall's Quilting*

Martingale®
19021 120th Ave. NE, Suite 102
Bothell, WA 98011 USA
ShopMartingale.com

McCall's Quilting, ISSN 1072-8395, is published bimonthly by Creative Crafts Group, LLC, 741 Corporate Circle, Suite A, Golden, CO, 80401, www.mccallsquilting.com.

Printed in China
17 16 15 14 13 12   8 7 6 5 4 3 2 1

Library of Congress Cataloging-in-Publication Data
Library of Congress Control Number: 2012014937

ISBN: 978-1-60468-206-9

Mission Statement

Dedicated to providing quality products and service to inspire creativity.

Credits

President & CEO: Tom Wierzbicki

Editor in Chief: Mary V. Green

Design Director: Paula Schlosser

Managing Editor: Karen Costello Soltys

Copy Editor: Marcy Heffernan

Production Manager: Regina Girard

Cover & Text Designer: Regina Girard

Illustrators: Laurel Strand,
Robin Strobel, and Connor Chin

Photographer: Brent Kane

Contents

Introduction

Although there's nothing like a lap or bed quilt for comfort and utility, quilters who want their homes to reflect their sewing passion have long relied on wall hangings to showcase their work. *McCall's Quilting and McCall's Quick Quilts* magazines have published many wall quilt patterns through the years, and our editorial team has established what we consider these essential elements of a successful wall quilt design:

• A wall quilt should be visually exciting, drawing the viewer in for a closer look. Lap and bed quilts may rely on long user exposure in order to exert their charm. But a wall quilt needs to make an impact quickly, as the viewer is walking past it or scanning a room.

• Wall quilts can be seasonal or strongly related to a particular decorating style, since quilters often prefer to change out wall hangings on a regular basis to refresh their decor.

• A quilted wall hanging is a great place to try an unusual or challenging technique. The limited size of such a project makes these fun methods appealing and achievable, even for beginning or time-challenged quilters.

• Nature themes are particular favorites among quilters for wall decor. After all, what room isn't improved by a vase (or a little quilt) full of lovely flowers?

• Wall hangings make wonderful gift quilts, and quilters *love* to create for family and friends.

In other words, a wall hanging quilt is the perfect place to try out new designs, styles, and skills, packing a lot of quilting fun into a limited amount of time. Whether your decorating style is traditional or contemporary, elegant or homey, neutral or aglow with color, there are projects in this book perfect for brightening any room in the house at any season of the year. Sit back, relax, and spend some time looking over these beautiful photographs and helpful patterns. You're sure to find your next wall quilt, ready to make and to enjoy.

– From the editors at

Spring Fling

Brighten the darkest corner of any room with a splash of quilted color. Despite a wall of windows, this sunroom had an interior corner perfect for displaying a small quilt. It's like sunshine on the wall!

Designed by JoBeth Simons; machine quilted by Ardis Young

•

Finished quilt size: 36½" x 48½"

•

Number of blocks and finished size: 4 Double Pinwheel blocks, 8" x 8"

Planning

JoBeth placed her flower petals randomly for a whimsical feel and appliquéd them by hand. The appliqué patterns are on page 10, and do not include seam allowances. You can use the appliqué method of your choice; for hand appliqué, add seam allowances when you cut out the fabric pieces. For fusible appliqué, reverse the patterns before using them. Use an accurate ¼" seam allowance throughout to ensure the pieced border fits well.

Materials

Yardage is based on 42"-wide fabric unless noted otherwise.

Orange mottled print for Double Pinwheel blocks, pieced border, and binding	1⅛ yards
White print for Four Patch blocks, Double Pinwheel blocks, and pieced border	1⅜ yards
Assorted orange prints for Four Patch blocks and appliqué	⅞ yard *total*
Assorted yellow prints for Four Patch blocks and appliqué	¾ yard *total*
Assorted red prints for Four Patch blocks and appliqué	¾ yard *total*
Assorted green prints for Double Pinwheel blocks and leaves	½ yard *total*
Green dotted print for Double Pinwheel blocks and vines	½ yard
Fabric for backing	1⅝ yards*
Batting	42" x 54"
Template plastic	
Paper-backed fusible web (optional)	
⅜"-wide bias bar (optional)	

Based on 42" usable width.

Cutting

Appliqué patterns A–G are on page 10.
Cut pieces in the order listed.

From the assorted orange prints, cut:
- 4 sets of 2 matching squares, 4⅞" x 4⅞"; cut in half diagonally to yield 4 half-square triangles (16 total)
- 3 matched sets of 1 *each* of A, B, C, D, and E
- 40 squares, 2½" x 2½"
- 3 of F

From the assorted yellow prints, cut:
- 4 matched sets of 1 *each* of A, B, C, D, and E
- 40 squares 2½" x 2½"
- 3 of F

From the white print, cut:
- 2 strips, 4½" x 32½"*
- 2 strips, 4½" x 20½"*
- 4 squares, 5¼" x 5¼"; cut into quarters diagonally to yield 16 quarter-square triangles
- 52 rectangles, 2½" x 4½"
- 40 squares, 2½" x 2½"

From the assorted red prints, cut:
- 3 matched sets of 1 *each* of A, B, C, D, and E
- 40 squares, 2½" x 2½"
- 4 of F

From the orange mottled print, cut:
- 5 strips, 2½" x 42"
- 104 squares, 2½" x 2½"

From the assorted green prints, cut:
- 4 squares, 5¼" x 5¼"; cut into quarters diagonally to yield 16 quarter-square triangles
- 12 of G
- 10 of G reversed

From the green dotted print, cut:
- 1¼"-wide bias strips, enough to yield 120" in length
- 1 square, 5¼" x 5¼"; cut into quarters diagonally to yield 4 quarter-square triangles

Border strips are cut to exact length.

Piecing the Four Patch Blocks

1. Stitch together two yellow, one orange, and one white print 2½" squares to make Four Patch block A. Repeat to make 20 total.

Four-Patch block A.
Make 20.

2. In the same manner, make 20 total of Four Patch block B using two red, one orange, and one white print 2½" squares.

Four-Patch block B.
Make 20.

Piecing the Border Blocks and Units

1. Sew together a white and a green print 5¼" quarter-square triangle along their short edges as shown. Press the seam allowances toward the green fabric. Sew the resulting pieced triangle to an orange print 4⅞" half-square triangle to make a pieced square. Make four sets of four matching units.

Make 4 sets
of 4 matching units.

2. Stitch together four matching units from step 1 to make a Double Pinwheel block. Repeat to make a total of four blocks.

Double Pinwheel block.
Make 4.

3. Draw a diagonal line on the wrong side of an orange mottled 2½" square. Place the marked square on a white 2½" x 4½" rectangle, right sides together, aligning the raw edges. Stitch on the drawn line; leaving a ¼" seam allowance, trim away and discard the excess fabric. Open and press. Repeat the process on the opposite end of the rectangle to make a pieced rectangle. Make 52.

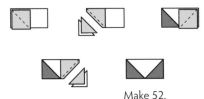

Make 52.

4. Sew eight pieced rectangles together side by side. Repeat to make four of these pieced strips. Sew the strips to opposite sides of the white 4½" x 32½" strips to make two long border strips.

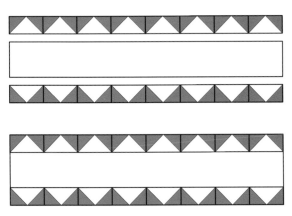

Make 2.

5. In a similar manner, make four short pieced strips by sewing the remaining pieced rectangles together in sets of five. Sew these strips to the 4½" x 20½" white strips.

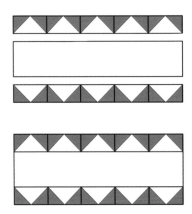

Make 2.

6. Sew the green 1¼"-wide bias strips together end to end. Fold the bias strip in half, wrong sides together. Stitch ⅜" from the fold. Trim the seam allowances to ⅛". Press the resulting tube flat, centering the seam allowances along the back so raw edges aren't visible from the front. Using a ⅜"-wide bias bar makes pressing faster and easier. Cut the bias tube into two vines 36" long and two vines 24" long.

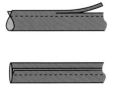

Assembling the Quilt Top

Refer to the assembly diagram on page 10 for the following steps, watching orientation and placement.

1. Using the seams as a placement guide, position a 36" vine and shapes A–G reverse in alphabetical order on a long pieced border strip. Appliqué all the pieces in place. Make two. In a similar manner, appliqué the two short border strips.

2. Sew the Four Patch blocks into eight rows of five blocks each.

3. Stitch the long appliquéd border strips to the sides of the quilt top. Sew the Double Pinwheel blocks to the ends of the short appliquéd border strips. Sew these strips to the top and bottom of the quilt top.

Assembly diagram

Quilting and Finishing

1. Layer, baste, and quilt as desired. Ardis machine quilted diagonal lines across the Four Patch blocks and arcs in each square. She quilted a small flower motif in the orange triangles of the pieced borders and a small meandering pattern in the white areas of the pieced borders.
2. Bind the quilt with the orange mottled 2½"-wide strips.

> Patterns do not include seam allowances. Add seam allowances for hand appliqué; reverse patterns for fusible appliqué.

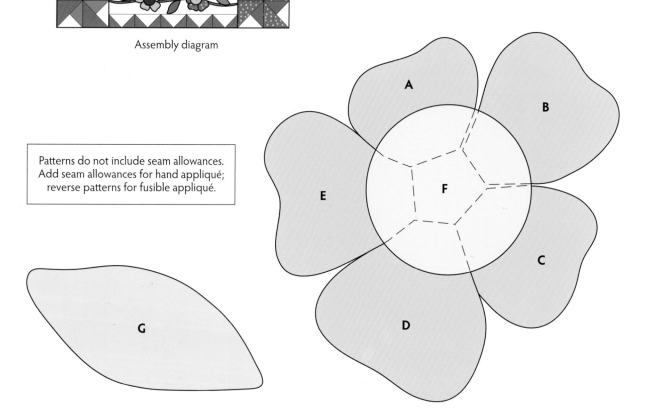

Lantern Light

Each year, the Chinese New Year's festivities conclude with the Lantern Festival, marking the first full moon of the new year. Celebrate with this appealing little quilt, made with an assortment of Asian-themed prints.

Designed by Laurie Bevan; machine quilted by Julie Gutierrez of Quilter's Paradise

•

Finished quilt size: 39½" x 48½"

•

Number of blocks and finished size:
3 Large Lantern blocks, 8" x 10"
16 Small Lantern blocks, 6½" x 8"
4 World's Fair blocks, 6½" x 8"

Planning

Elegant but simple, Laurie's quilt shows the effect that can be created by using the same block in two different sizes.

The center of the quilt is assembled in three sections, which are then stitched together. Refer to the assembly diagram for seaming order.

Be sure to use a precise ¼" seam allowance throughout the construction so that the pieced Lantern border fits accurately.

Materials

Yardage is based on 42"-wide fabric unless noted otherwise; a fat quarter is an 18" x 20" cut of fabric.

Black-and-coral large-scale floral for World's Fair blocks and setting rectangles	1 yard
Cream-and-gold floral for blocks	⅞ yard
Black-and-gold small-scale print for blocks and binding	⅞ yard
Black solid for blocks and inner border	½ yard
Black-and-gold floral for blocks	½ yard
Red-and-cream floral for blocks	½ yard
Red-and-cream print for blocks	1 fat quarter
Black-and-gold print for blocks	1 fat quarter
Fabric for backing	2¾ yards
Batting	44" x 53"

Cutting

From the cream-and-gold floral, cut:
- 4 strips, 2½" x 42"*
- 12 rectangles, 1¾" x 3"
- 12 squares, 3" x 3"
- 64 squares, 2½" x 2½"

From the black solid, cut:
- 1 strip, 3" x 42"*
- 2 strips, 1¼" x 31"*
- 2 strips, 1¼" x 26½"*
- 4 rectangles, 1¾" x 3½"

From the black-and-gold small-scale print, cut:
- 1 strip, 3" x 42"*
- 2 rectangles, 1¾" x 3½"
- 16 squares, 3¾" x 3¾"
- 5 strips, 2½" x 42"

From the black-and-gold floral, cut:
- 4 rectangles, 3" x 8½"
- 16 rectangles, 2½" x 7"

From the red-and-cream floral, cut:
- 2 rectangles, 3" x 8½"
- 16 rectangles, 2½" x 7"

From the red-and-cream print, cut:
- 2 rectangles, 3" x 8½"
- 8 rectangles, 2½" x 7"

From the black-and-gold print, cut:
- 1 rectangle, 3" x 8½"
- 8 rectangles, 2½" x 7"

Cut first.

From the black-and-coral large-scale floral, cut:
- 4 rectangles, 7" x 8½"
- 1 strip, 2¼" x 10½"
- 1 strip, 2¾" x 10¼"
- 1 rectangle, 6½" x 10¼"
- 1 strip, 2½" x 8½"
- 1 strip, 3½" x 12½"
- 1 strip, 4¼" x 12½"
- 1 strip, 6¾" x 15¼"
- 1 strip, 2¾" x 8½"
- 1 rectangle, 8¼" x 12¾"
- 1 rectangle, 9¼" x 12¾"

Piecing the Blocks

1. Stitch two cream-and-gold floral 1¾" x 3" rectangles to a black solid 1¾" x 3½" rectangle to make a pieced strip. Make four. In the same manner, use cream-and-gold 1¾" x 3" rectangles and a black-and-gold small-scale print 1¾" x 3½" rectangle to make a pieced strip. Make two.

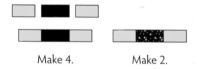

Make 4. Make 2.

2. Sew a cream-and-gold 2½"-wide strip to each side of the black-and-gold small-scale print 3"-wide strip. In the same manner, sew two cream-and-gold strips to a black solid 3"-wide strip. Press all seam allowances toward the black strips. Cut 16 segments, 1½" wide, from each strip set.

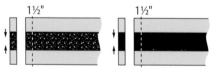

Make 1 of each strip set.
Cut 16 segments.

3. Draw a diagonal line on the wrong side of a cream-and-gold 3" square. Place a marked square on a black-and-gold floral 3" x 8½" rectangle, right sides together, aligning raw edges. Stitch on the drawn line. Trim away and discard the excess fabric; press open. Repeat on the opposite end to make a large black lantern unit. Make four.

   Repeat the process with cream-and-gold 3" squares and a red-and-cream floral 3" x 8½" rectangle to make a large red lantern unit. Make two.

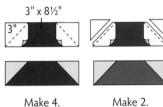

Make 4.   Make 2.

4. Using the cream-and-gold 2½" squares and the red floral and black floral 2½" x 7" rectangles, make 16 red and 16 black small lantern units in the same manner as for the large lantern units.

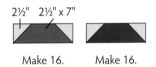

Make 16.   Make 16.

5. To make the large Lantern blocks, stitch together two black solid and cream-and-gold pieced strips from step 1, two large black lantern units, and a red-and-cream print 3" x 8½" rectangle. Make two. Repeat, using two small-scale print and cream-and-gold pieced strips, two large red lantern units, and a black-and-gold print 3" x 8½" rectangle.

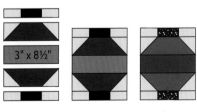

Make 2.   Make 1.

6. In a similar manner, make small Lantern blocks using the pieced strips from step 2, the small lantern units from step 4, and black or red 2½" x 7" rectangles. Make eight small Lantern blocks with black middle rows and eight with red middle rows.

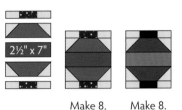

Make 8.   Make 8.

7. Using the same method as in step 3, mark four black-and-gold small-scale print 3¾" squares and stitch them to a black-and-coral large-scale floral 7" x 8½" rectangle; press and trim the seam allowances. Repeat to make four total World's Fair blocks.

Make 4.

Assembling the Quilt Top

Refer to the assembly diagram, opposite, and the photo (page 11) for the following steps.

1. Stitch black-and-coral strips and a rectangle to the black large Lantern block to make the left center section. In a similar manner, sew strips, rectangles and blocks together to make the remaining center sections. Following the seaming order, sew the sections together to make the quilt center.

2. Sew black solid 1¼" x 31" strips to the quilt sides. Stitch black solid 1¼" x 26½" strips to the top and bottom of the quilt.

3. To make a side lantern border, stitch together two red and two black small Lantern blocks end to end, alternating as shown. Make one of each arrangement and sew them to the quilt sides. To make the top and bottom border, sew together two red and two black small Lantern blocks side by side, alternating the colors. Make one of each arrangement. Add a World's Fair block to each end of these border strips. Sew the borders to the top and bottom of the quilt.

Quilting and Finishing

1. Layer, baste, and quilt. Julie used gold metallic thread to machine quilt elongated hexagons in the lanterns and a flame motif on the cream patches of the lantern blocks. She stitched a vertical serpentine pattern on the top and bottom of each lantern, and an Asian wave motif to fill the black-and-coral patches.

2. Bind the quilt with the black-and-gold small-scale print 2½"-wide strips.

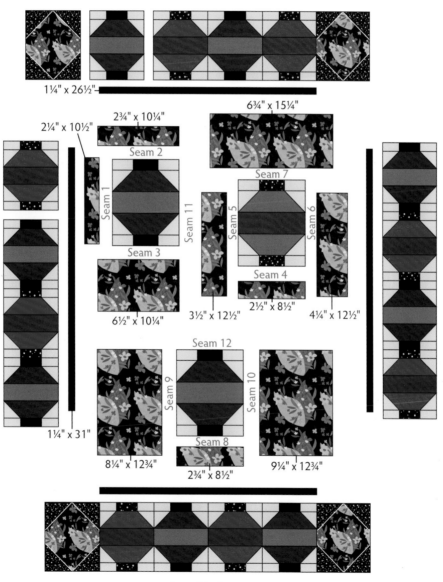

Assembly diagram

Create a work of art with graphic tone-on-tone prints, batiks, or solids. A palette of subtly sophisticated color, pattern, and visual texture is shown off to best effect in this easy-to-piece modern wall hanging.

*Designed by Jan Douglas;
machine quilted by Barbara Persing*

•

Finished quilt size: 68" x 68"

•

Number of blocks and finished size:
25 blocks, 11" x 11"

Materials

Yardage is based on 42"-wide fabric, unless otherwise noted.

8 assorted green prints	1 fat quarter *each*
6 assorted brown prints	1 fat quarter *each*
7 assorted purple prints	1 fat quarter *each*
9 assorted red prints	1 fat quarter *each*
5 assorted gold prints	1 fat quarter *each*
3 assorted dark prints (#1, #2, and #4) for border	⅞ yard *each*
1 dark print (#3) for border and binding	1⅜ yards
Fabric for backing	4⅜ yards
Batting	72" x 72"
Template plastic	

Planning

Thirty-nine fabrics are used in this quilt. The eight greens range from moss green to bluish green to bright green; the six browns range from tan to taupe to dark brown; the seven purples from violet to rose; the nine reds are warmer reds, so that they contrast sufficiently with the purples; the five golds from yellow to dark gold; and the four dark border fabrics are brown or rust prints on a black background. We strongly recommend the use of a design wall for arranging the blocks.

Because the half-square triangles are rotary cut from squares, you'll end up with twice the necessary number of triangles from many of the fabrics. You may wish to piece a second quilt top from the leftover fabrics (additional yardage for borders will be necessary), or use the extras to create coordinating room accessories such as pillows or a table runner.

Even though the smaller triangles in the block piecing would typically be cut as quarter-square triangles, we instruct you to cut all block triangles as half-square triangles so you'll be able to complete the cutting from a fat quarter rather than additional yardage. Take care to avoid stretching their bias edges.

In order for the pieced border to fit and the corners to miter perfectly, accurate sewing of all ¼" seam allowances is necessary. As with the quilt shown, the instructions are for using a different brown-and-black print for each pieced border corner.

Cutting

From *each* of the 35 assorted fat quarters, cut:
- 1 square, 11⅞" x 11⅞"; cut in half diagonally to yield 2 half-square triangles
- 1 square, 8⅝" x 8⅝"; cut in half diagonally to yield 2 half-square triangles

From *each* of the 4 assorted dark prints for border, cut:
- 2 strips, 6¾" x 24¾" (8 total)
- 1 square, 13¾" x 13¾"; cut into quarters diagonally to yield 4 quarter-square triangles (16 total)
- 1 square, 11⅞" x 11⅞"; cut in half diagonally to yield 2 half-square triangles (8 total)
- 1 square, 8⅝" x 8⅝"; cut in half diagonally to yield 2 half-square triangles (8 total)

From the dark print #3, cut:
- 7 strips, 2½" x 42

Piecing the Blocks

1. Label each of your fabrics with its color family and number; assign numbers arbitrarily within color families. Referring to the fabric planning diagram, arrange the block fabrics on your design wall.

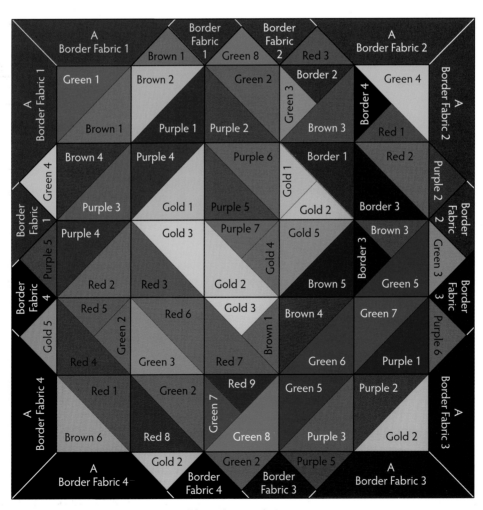

Fabric planning diagram

2. Piece the blocks as shown. Make 25 total.

Make 16. Make 9.

KEEPING COLOR ORDER

Rather than chain piecing, it's best to piece the blocks one at a time and replace them in your layout as you go.

Assembling the Quilt Top

Refer to the assembly diagram, right, for the following steps.

1. Sew together five rows of five blocks each. Sew the rows together.
2. Cut a 6¾" square of template plastic. Cut the square in half diagonally. Place the resulting triangle template at the end of a border strip and mark a cutting line. Repeat at the opposite end of the strip, flipping the template so both ends are trimmed with angles in opposite directions.

24¾"

6¾"

11¼"

Trim. Trim.

3. Before piecing the border strips, study the fabric arrangement (see fabric planning diagram, left) and read "Aligning Border Triangles" above right. Working on one border at a time, first stitch together the five triangles for the middle of the border strip, trimming the corners of the oversized triangles as shown.

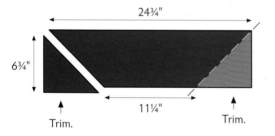

Trim.

Trim. Trim.

ALIGNING BORDER TRIANGLES

To align the triangles for piecing, mark match points on the wrong side of the triangle fabric by marking the intersecting ¼" seam-allowance lines at the corners to be matched (see the dots in the diagram).

4. In the same manner, add a trapezoid A piece to each end of the border strip, ensuring that the A pieces match the border-print triangles nearest them.
5. Repeat steps 1–3 to make four pieced border strips. Sew a border strip to each side of the quilt, starting and stopping ¼" from the corners and making sure to use the same color A trapezoid on the two adjacent sides of each corner. Sew the mitered-corner seams, referring to "Borders with Mitered Corners" (page 78); and press the seam allowances open.

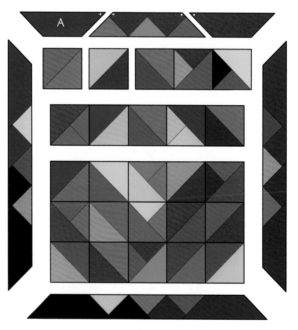

Assembly diagram

Quilting and Finishing

1. Layer, baste, and quilt. Barbara machine quilted, covering each band of color with a large, flowing, meandering pattern.
2. Bind the quilt with the dark print #3 strips.

Iris and Friends

Daffodils, irises, and tulips make the perfect
springtime—or anytime!—gift for your mom or best friend.

*Designed by Cheryl Almgren Taylor;
machine quilted by Cheryl Winslow*

•

Finished quilt size: 42¼" x 48¼"

Planning

Mottled fabrics add dimension and realism without extra effort. Notice that stems, leaves, and petals aren't placed identically from flower to flower, making each one unique, just as in nature. Feel free to create your own springtime garden as you wish. You may wish to label the violet and purple prints to avoid confusion with similar colors.

Materials

Yardage is based on 42"-wide fabric unless noted otherwise.

Light-violet tone-on-tone print and yellow checked print for four-patch units	¼ yard *each*
Light-green mottled print for appliquéd background strips	⅝ yard
Medium-green mottled print for stems and leaves	½ yard
Bright-yellow mottled print for daffodils and tulips	¼ yard
Light-yellow mottled print and bright-yellow tone-on-tone print for daffodils	7" x 8" piece *each*
Light-olive mottled print for appliquéd background strip	⅜ yard
Medium-olive mottled print for stems and leaves	¼ yard
Dark-violet mottled print for irises, inner border, and binding	⅞ yard
Medium-violet mottled print and bright-violet mottled print for irises	8" x 12" piece *each*
Medium-yellow tone-on-tone print for tulips	8" x 8" piece
Dark-purple dotted print and white tone-on-tone print for four-patch strips	¼ yard *each*
Light-purple tone-on-tone print for four-patch strips	⅜ yard
Medium-green dotted print for outer border	1½ yards
Fabric for backing	2⅞ yards
Batting	50" x 56" piece
Paper-backed fusible web	2 yards

Cutting

From both the light-violet tone-on-tone print and yellow checked print, cut:
- 28 squares, 2" x 2"

From the light-green mottled print, cut:
- 2 strips, 8¼" x 30¼"

From the light-olive mottled print, cut:
- 1 strip, 8¼" x 30¼"

From the dark-violet mottled print, cut:
- 4 strips, 1¾" x 42"*
- 5 strips, 2½" x 42"*

From the light-purple tone-on-tone print, cut:
- 6 squares, 5½" x 5½"; cut into quarters diagonally to yield 24 quarter-square triangles
- 4 squares, 3" x 3"; cut in half diagonally to yield 8 half-square triangles

From the dark-purple dotted print, cut:
- 32 rectangles, 1½" x 2½"

From the white tone-on-tone print, cut:
- 28 rectangles, 1½" x 2½"

From the medium-green dotted print, cut on the *lengthwise grain*:
- 4 strips, 5¼" x 46"

*Cut these before appliqués.

Making the Appliquéd Strips

Appliqué patterns are on pages 24 and 25 are printed reversed and without seam allowances for use with paper-backed fusible web.

1. Trace patterns A–P onto the paper side of the fusible web. Cut the shapes apart, leaving ¼" beyond the drawn lines. Following the manufacturer's instructions, fuse the shapes to the wrong side of the appropriate fabrics; cut them out on the drawn lines.

2. Finger-press a light-green mottled 8¼" x 30¼" strip in half lengthwise and widthwise; use the folds as placement guides. Referring to the illustration below and photo on page 20, position shapes A–F reverse. Following the manufacturer's instructions, fuse the shapes in place to make the daffodil strip.

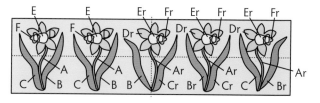

Make 1.

3. In a similar manner, fuse the G–N reverse shapes to the light-olive 8¼" x 30¼" strip to make the iris strip.

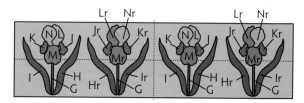

Make 1.

4. For the tulip strip, fuse the A–C reverse and O and P shapes to the remaining light-green 8¼" x 30¼" strip as shown.

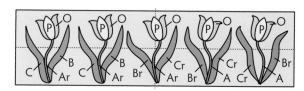

Make 1.

5. With matching thread, machine stitch the edges of the stems using a straight stitch, and blanket stitch the remaining appliqué edges on all three appliquéd strips.

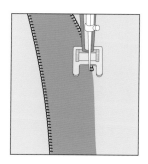

Machine blanket stitch.

Making the Four-Patch Strips

1. Using the light-violet and yellow-checked 2" squares, sew two rows of two squares each. Join the rows to make a four-patch unit. Make 14.

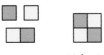

Make 14.

2. To make a four-patch strip, sew together seven four-patch units and 12 light-purple 5½" quarter-square triangles as shown. Sew light-purple 3" half-square triangles to the corners. Make two.

Make 2.

3. Join eight purple-dotted and seven white 1½" x 2½" rectangles along their short edges, alternating them. Make four of these strips and sew them to the long sides of the four-patch strips, centering the four-patch strips between them. If necessary, trim the ends of the purple-and-white strips even with the four-patch strips.

Assembling the Quilt Top

1. Stitch together the appliquéd strips and four-patch strips, alternating them.
2. Sew two of the dark-violet mottled 1¾"-wide strips to the quilt sides; trim the ends even with the top and bottom of the quilt top. Stitch the remaining strips to the top and bottom of the quilt; trim the strips even with the sides of the quilt top.

3. Sew the green dotted strips to the quilt sides; trim the strips even. Add the remaining green dotted strips to the top and bottom; trim the strips even.

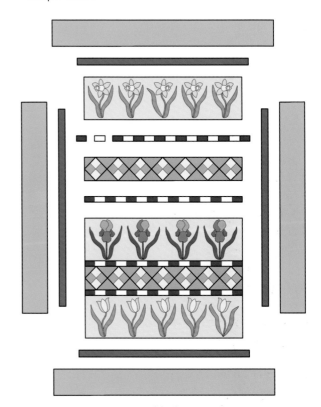

Assembly diagram

Quilting and Finishing

1. Layer, baste, and quilt. Cheryl machine quilted the appliquéd strips, four-patch strips, and inner border in the ditch. She quilted the four-patch strips with a diagonal ¾" grid, outline quilted the appliquéd shapes, and filled the backgrounds with swirls and meandering feathers. The iris beards she quilted with yellow thread, and the inner and outer borders feature feather quilting.
2. Bind the quilt with the dark-violet mottled 2½"-wide strips.

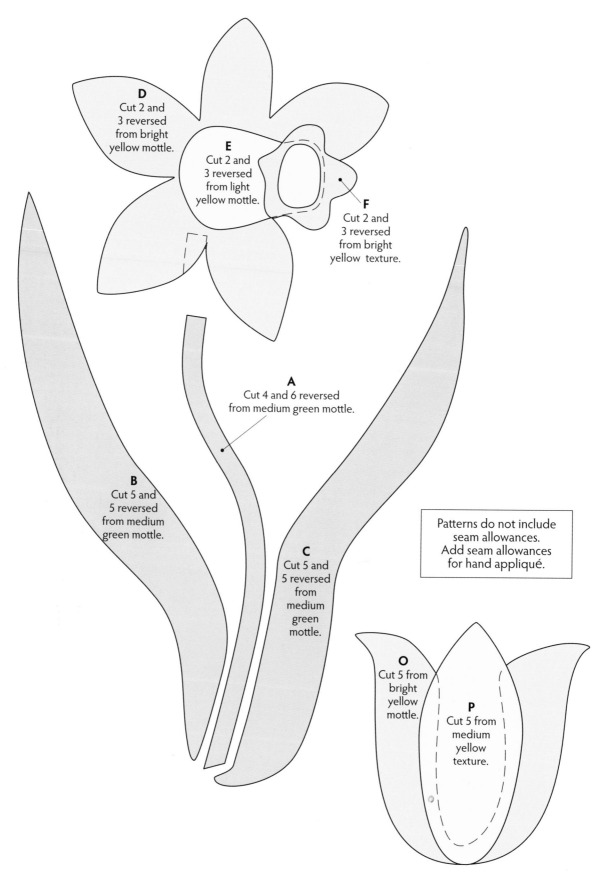

D
Cut 2 and
3 reversed
from bright
yellow mottle.

E
Cut 2 and
3 reversed
from light
yellow mottle.

F
Cut 2 and
3 reversed
from bright
yellow texture.

A
Cut 4 and 6 reversed
from medium green mottle.

B
Cut 5 and
5 reversed
from medium
green mottle.

C
Cut 5 and
5 reversed
from
medium
green
mottle.

Patterns do not include
seam allowances.
Add seam allowances
for hand appliqué.

O
Cut 5 from
bright
yellow
mottle.

P
Cut 5 from
medium
yellow
texture.

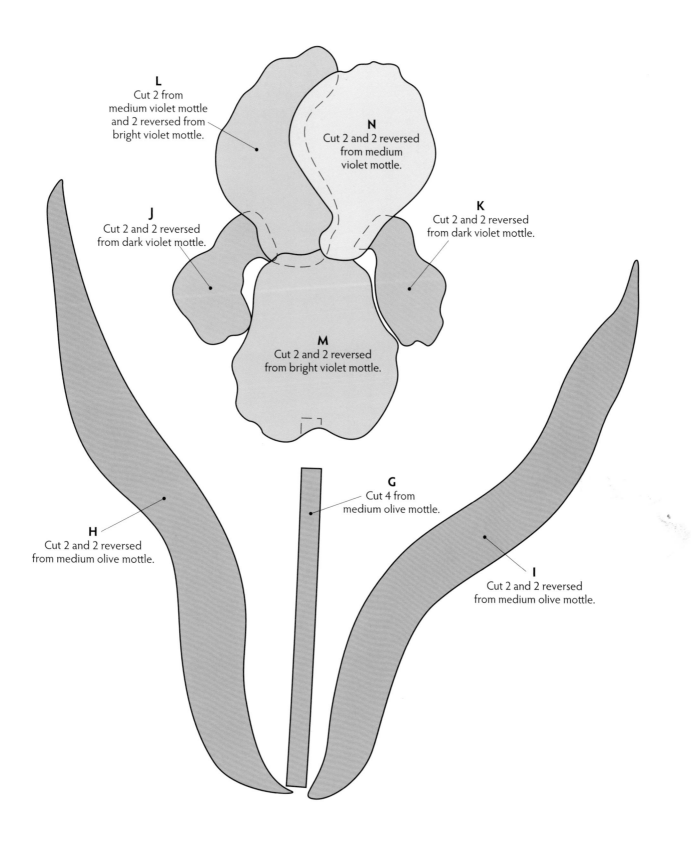

L
Cut 2 from
medium violet mottle
and 2 reversed from
bright violet mottle.

N
Cut 2 and 2 reversed
from medium
violet mottle.

J
Cut 2 and 2 reversed
from dark violet mottle.

K
Cut 2 and 2 reversed
from dark violet mottle.

M
Cut 2 and 2 reversed
from bright violet mottle.

G
Cut 4 from
medium olive mottle.

H
Cut 2 and 2 reversed
from medium olive mottle.

I
Cut 2 and 2 reversed
from medium olive mottle.

Shimmering Squares

Free your inner artist with a bold, bright wall hanging, perfect for contemporary interiors. Fabric selection and placement tips will help guide you in creating your own version of this dramatic design.

Designed by Renée Peterson

•

Finished quilt size: 60½" x 60½"

•

Number of blocks and finished sizes:
64 Brave World Variation blocks, 5" x 5"
52 Square-in-a-Square blocks, 3½" x 3½"

Materials
Yardage is based on 42"-wide fabric unless noted otherwise.

Assorted dark prints and batiks for blocks and pieced second and fourth borders	3 to 3½ yards *total*
Assorted light prints and batiks for blocks and pieced second and fourth borders	1¾ to 2¼ yards *total*
Green mottled print for first border	⅜ yard
Dark-blue mottled print for third border	½ yard
Purple striped print for binding	¾ yard
Fabric for backing	4 yards
Batting	65" x 65"

Planning
Renée's striking quilt combines a dazzling array of prints and visual textures with careful selection and placement of values (dark and light fabrics) to make this successful design.

- Divide your fabrics into darks and lights, making sure you have some brights included in each value group.
- Make sure you have a range of values within each group, such as very light to medium light, and medium dark to very dark.
- Use the lightest lights in the corners of the Square-in-a-Square blocks ("Piecing the Blocks and Border Units," page 28, step 2).

- Use the darkest darks and darkest or brightest lights to piece the outer-border units.
- Notice in the quilt shown that each block has a dark and a light fabric. Some fabric pairs are very close in value, while others have strong contrast. The brights are sprinkled around the quilt center, adding spice and sparkle.
- Remember as you choose fabric pairs for different areas of your quilt that value is relative—the apparent value of any fabric is affected by its immediate neighbors. A fabric looks dark when placed next to a lighter one; the same fabric seems light next to a darker fabric. The intensity or brightness of a fabric is affected in the same way by its surroundings.

Cutting

From the assorted dark prints and dark batiks, cut:
- 64 pieces, 6" x 6½"; cut each piece into:*
  1 half-square triangle, 5⅞" x 5⅞"
  1 square, 3" x 3"
- 52 squares, 3" x 3"
- 30 squares, 4⅝" x 4⅝"; cut in half diagonally to yield 60 half-square triangles

From the assorted light prints and light batiks, cut:
- 52 sets of 2 matching squares, 2⅝" x 2⅝"; cut in half diagonally to yield 208 half-square triangles
- 64 squares, 3⅜" x 3⅜"; cut in half diagonally to yield 128 half-square triangles
- 30 squares, 4⅝" x 4⅝"; cut in half diagonally to yield 60 half-square triangles

From the green mottled print, cut:
- 2 strips, 1½" x 40½"
- 3 inner-border strips, 1½" x 42"

From the dark-blue mottled print, cut:
- 6 border strips, 2¼" x 42"

From the purple striped print, cut:
- 7 binding strips, 2½" x 42"

* You can cut a matching dark triangle and square for a Brave World Variation block from a 6" x 6½" rectangle; as shown below.

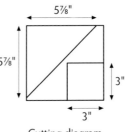

Cutting diagram

Piecing the Blocks and Border Units

1. Sew two matching light 3⅜" half-square triangles to a dark 3" square. Add a matching dark 5⅞" half-square triangle to complete the Brave World Variation block. Make 64 total.

Brave World block.
Make 64 total.

2. Stitch four matching light 2⅝" half-square triangles to the sides of a dark 3" square to make a Square-in-a-Square block. Make 52 total.

Square-in-a-Square block.
Make 52 total.

3. Sew together a dark and a light 4⅝" half-square triangle to make a pieced square. Make 60 total.

Make 60 total.

Assembling the Quilt Top

Refer to the assembly diagram for the following steps, watching the orientation throughout. Use an accurate ¼" seam allowance so the pieced borders fit well.

1. Arrange eight rows of eight Brave World Variation blocks each on a design wall or other flat surface. Once you're satisfied with the arrangement, sew the rows together.
2. Stitch the two green mottled 40½"-long strips to the sides of the quilt top. Join the three green mottled 42"-long strips end to end, and from them cut a top and a bottom border strip, 42½" long. Sew these strips to the top and bottom of the quilt.
3. Join 12 Square-in-a-Square blocks. Make two pieced strips and sew them to the sides of the quilt top. Stitch together 14 Square-in-a-Square blocks. Make two pieced strips and sew them to the top and bottom of the quilt.
4. Sew the dark-blue mottled 2¼"-wide strips together end to end. From this long strip, cut two borders 49½" long and sew them to the sides of the quilt top. Cut two 53"-long strips from the remaining long strip and sew them to the top and bottom of the quilt.
5. For the pieced outer border, stitch together 14 pieced squares to make a pieced strip; make two. Sew these pieced border strips to the sides of the quilt top. Sew together 16 pieced squares to make a pieced strip; make two. Sew these pieced border strips to the top and bottom of the quilt.

Quilting and Finishing

1. Layer, baste, and quilt. Renée hand quilted in the ditch around all the patches and borders. In the Brave World Variation blocks, she quilted a diagonal line through each small square and small triangle, and outline quilted the corner of the large triangle 1" from the seams. In the Square-in-a-Square blocks she quilted through the squares, with the line extending through the dark-blue border. The outer border features a zigzag, 1" from the seams.
2. Bind the quilt with the striped purple 2½"-wide strips.

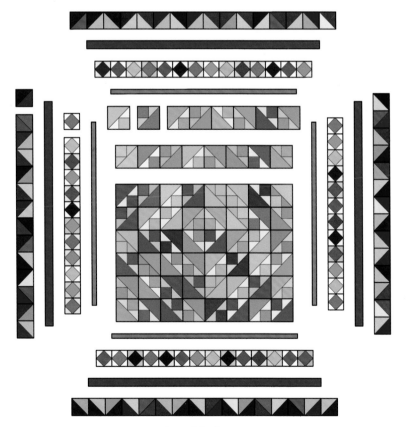

Assembly diagram

Asian Elegance

Simplicity, serenity, and artful composition are the hallmarks of Asian design. Inspired by the restrained floral arrangements, perfectly raked white sand, and paneled screens of a Japanese garden, this project creates an island of Eastern tranquility in even the busiest of environments.

Designed by Vicky Wozniak

•

Finished quilt size: 48" x 48"

•

Number of blocks and finished size:
1 Appliquéd Fan block, 24½" x 24½"

Planning, Cutting, and Marking
The fan is pieced from 6 fabrics labeled #1–#6, from lightest to darkest, listed in "Materials" below. The fan base is rotary cut and pieced before being appliquéd to the block background.

Materials
Yardage is based on 42"-wide fabric unless noted otherwise.

Black solid for fan base, borders, and binding	1⅝ yards
Cream-and-gold print for setting triangles	1⅜ yards
Assorted green mottled prints and batiks for pieced border, stems, leaves, and calyxes	1 yard *total*
Beige print for fan strip #1	⅛ yard
Light-gold print for fan strip #2 and border corners	¼ yard
Medium-gold mottled print for fan strip #3 and fan background	⅞ yard
Purple-and-green batik for fan strip #4	⅛ yard
Purple fruit print for fan strip #5 and pieced border	⅝ yard
Purple-and-black print for fan strip #6	⅛ yard
Dark-rose mottled print for rosebuds	¼ yard
Fabric for backing	3¼ yards
Batting	52" x 52"
⅜"-wide flat black lace	¾ yard
Packaged ¼"-wide double-fold black bias tape	3½ yards
Template plastic	
¼" bias bar (optional)	
Metallic gold thread for hand quilting and embroidery	

Cutting

Appliqué and patchwork patterns are on pages 36 and 37. Appliqués C and E are printed without seam allowances.

From *each* of the beige print, purple-and-green batik, and purple-and-black print, cut:
• 1 strip, 1¾" x 42"

From the light-gold print, cut:
• 1 strip, 1¾" x 42"
• 4 squares, 3½" x 3½"

From the medium-gold mottled print, cut:
• 1 strip, 1¾" x 42"
• 1 square, 25" x 25"

From the purple fruit print, cut:
• 1 strip, 1¾" x 42"
• 8 strips, 3½" x 16¼"

From the black solid, cut:
• 2 strips, 1¾" x 42", cut on the *lengthwise grain**
• 6 strips, 1¾" x 52", cut on the *lengthwise grain**
• 1 of B
• 2 of C
• 12 rectangles, 1¾" x 3½"
• 5 strips, 2½" x 42"

From the cream-and-gold print, cut:
• 2 squares, 21" x 21"; cut in half diagonally to make 4 half-square triangles

From the assorted green mottled prints and batiks, cut:
• 1 set of 4 matching rectangles, 3⅛" x 3½"
• 12 of D
• 4 bias strips, 1" x 7"
• 4 bias strips, 1" x 7½"
• 4 bias strips, 1" x 8"
• 40 of E

From the dark-rose mottled print, cut:
• 12 squares 3" x 3"

Cut first.

Piecing and Appliquéing the Fan

1. Sew the 1¾"-wide strips of fabrics #1–#6 together to make a strip set. Press all seam allowances toward the darkest fabric.

2. Make a plastic template from pattern A. Lay the plastic template on the strip set with the narrow end of the template aligned with the lower raw edge of the light strip and the wide end even with the upper edge of the strip set; mark along the sides of the template with the marking tool of your choice. Rotate the template as shown to mark and cut 11 segments.

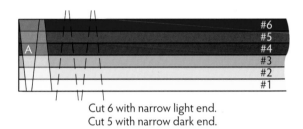

Cut 6 with narrow light end.
Cut 5 with narrow dark end.

3. Sew the segments together to make the fan as shown; press the seam allowances to the right, as indicated by the arrow.

4. Mark the center of the black circle B with the marking tool of your choice. Lay the fabric circle over the curve at the bottom of the fan, overlapping ½" for seam allowances.

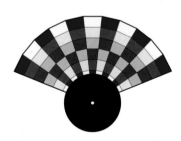

5. Align a rotary-cutting ruler with the right raw edge of the fan and with the marked center of the circle. With a rotary cutter, cut through the circle.

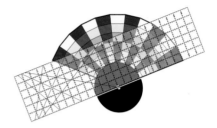

6. Align the ruler with the left raw edge of the fan and the marked center of the circle. Make a second cut through the circle. The circle is now in four pieces. Pull out the small side wedges and discard them.

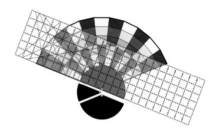

7. The remaining top wedge will be used as a base for the fan and the bottom wedge will be used as the fan tail. Mark and trim ½" from the curved edge of the fan tail as shown.

8. Finger-press the medium-gold 25" square in half diagonally in both directions; use the folds as a placement guide. Referring to the photo (page 30) and illustration above right, position the pieced fan, fan base, and tail on the gold square.

9. Using the method of your choice (see "Appliqué," page 75), appliqué the top curved edge of the fan, inserting the black lace ⅜"-wide strip along the fan edge at the same time. Appliqué the curved edges of the fan base and tail; do not appliqué the straight sides.

10. Using strips of ¼"-wide double-fold black bias tape, cover the straight raw edges of the fan, fan base, and tail. The bias tape will cross where the fan base and tail meet. Tuck the raw ends of the tape under and appliqué them in place.

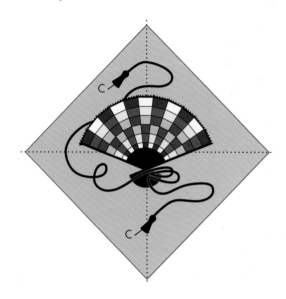

11. Using gold metallic thread, add running stitch and chain stitch details to the fan base and tail as shown.

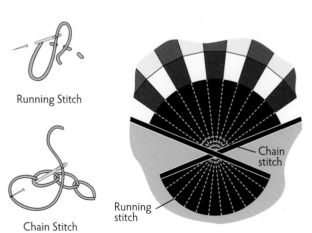

Running Stitch

Chain Stitch

Running stitch

Chain stitch

12. Position and appliqué the flowing ribbon and bow using ¼"-wide double-fold black bias tape. Appliqué a tassel C to each end of the ribbon. Using the gold metallic thread, stitch details on the tassels. (See pattern C for placement.)

Making the Pieced Borders

1. Sew two purple fruit print 3½" x 16¼" strips, two black solid 1¾" x 3½" rectangles, and one green 3⅛" x 3½" rectangle together. Make four. Sew a black 1¾" x 42" strip to the long side of a pieced strip; trim the ends of the black strip even with the pieced strip. Make two, one each for the top and bottom pieced borders.

Top/bottom border.
Make 2.

2. To finish the pieced side-border strips, sew a black 1¾" x 3½" rectangle and a light-gold 3½" square to each end of the two remaining pieced strips. Sew a black 1¾" x 52" strip to the long side of each pieced strip; trim the black strip even with the pieced strip.

Side border.
Make 2.

Assembling the Quilt Top

Refer to the assembly diagram, right, for the following steps.

1. Sew the cream-and-gold 21" half-square triangles to the sides of the appliquéd Fan block. (The triangles are cut oversized to allow the block to float and to allow for trimming the edges even.) To trim, lay the edge of your rotary-cutting ruler 1¼" from the point of the block and parallel with the quilt

edge, and cut away the excess. The quilt center should now measure 37⅛" square from raw edge to raw edge.

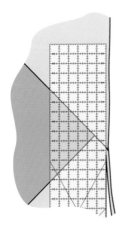

2. Sew the shorter pieced borders to the top and bottom of the quilt. Stitch the remaining pieced borders to the quilt sides. Sew the black 1¾" x 52" strips to the sides; trim the strips even with the top and bottom of the quilt. Stitch the remaining black strips to the top and bottom; trim the strips even with the sides of the quilt.

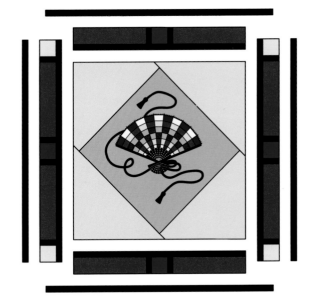

Appliquéing the Setting Triangles

1. To make the stems, fold the assorted green 1"-wide bias strips in half, wrong sides together. Stitch ¼" from the raw edge. Trim the seam allowance to ⅛". Press the tube flat, centering the seam allowances on the back so the raw edge isn't visible from the front. Using ¼" bias bar makes pressing faster and easier. Make 12 total.

2. Referring to the pattern placement illustration below, arrange and appliqué stems and leaves on the corners of the quilt top.

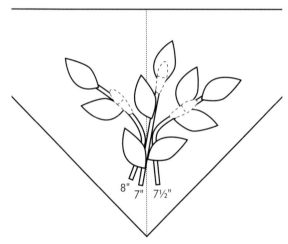

8" 7" 7½"

Asian Elegance pattern placement guide

3. To make 12 dimensional buds, fold the dark-rose 3" squares in half diagonally.

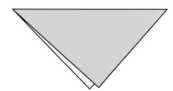

4. Fold the pointed corners in toward the center, overlapping as shown.

5. Roll back the right center edge of the top layer.

6. Fold the outside edges toward the center, overlapping as shown. Baste through the layers to hold the folds in place.

7. Fold the top and bottom edge of the calyx D pieces ¼" to wrong side and finger press.

8. Wrap the caylx around the folded bud, overlapping the raw edges on the back flat side of the rose and tack in place. Repeat all steps to make 12 dimensional rosebuds. Tack in place on the appliqué.

Quilting and Finishing

1. Layer and baste the quilt top for the quilting method of your choice. (See "Finishing" on page 79.) Using metallic gold thread, Vicky quilted in the ditch on the appliqués and pieced borders. She echo quilted the square shape of the quilt center.

2. Bind the quilt with the black solid 2½"-wide strips.

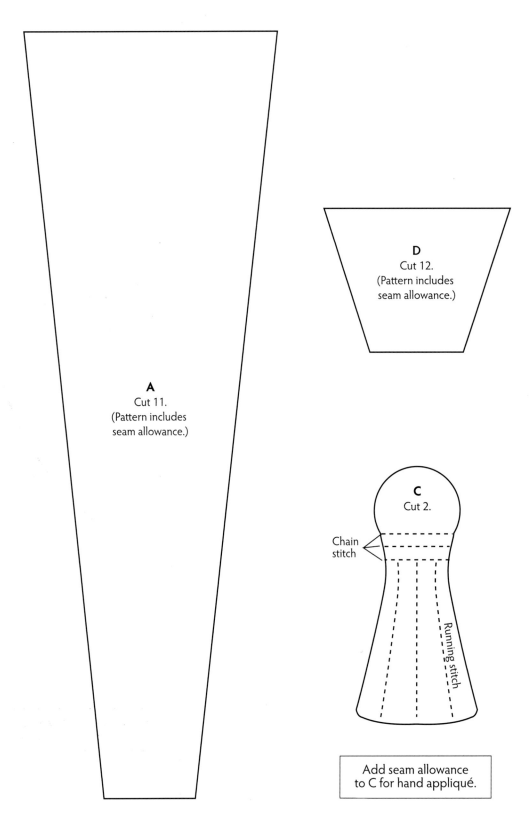

A
Cut 11.
(Pattern includes
seam allowance.)

D
Cut 12.
(Pattern includes
seam allowance.)

C
Cut 2.

Chain
stitch

Running stitch

Add seam allowance
to C for hand appliqué.

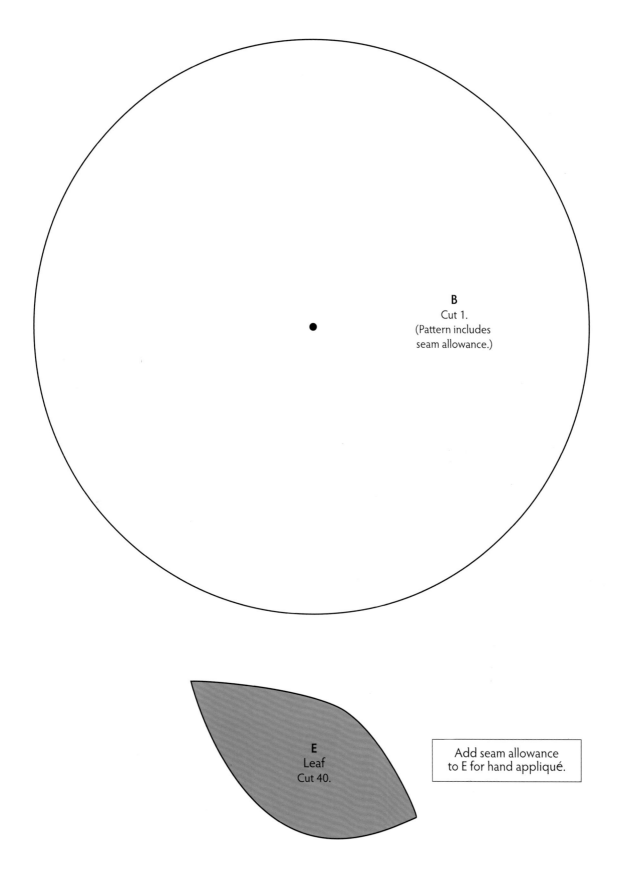

B
Cut 1.
(Pattern includes
seam allowance.)

E
Leaf
Cut 40.

Add seam allowance
to E for hand appliqué.

Let guests know they've entered a quilter's home by displaying some of your best work inside the main entry. This formal hallway is the perfect backdrop for a traditional quilt design featuring contemporary fabrics.

Designed by Cindy Lammon

•

Finished quilt size: 42½" x 42½"

Materials

Yardage is based on 42"-wide fabric unless noted otherwise.

Navy floral for star	¼ yard
Coral polka-dot and gray-and-red prints for star	⅜ yard *each*
Red print and aqua print for star	½ yard *each*
Navy print and peach print for star	⅝ yard *each*
Dark-gray solid for background	1⅛ yards
Orange-and-pink striped print for bias binding	¾ yard
Fabric for backing	3 yards
Batting	52" x 52"

Cutting

Cut in the order listed.

From the navy floral, cut:
• 1 strip, 2½" x 42"

From the coral polka-dot print, cut:
• 2 strips, 2½" x 42"

From the gray-and-red print, cut:
• 3 strips, 2½" x 42"

From the red print, cut:
• 4 strips, 2½" x 42"

From the aqua print, cut:
• 5 strips, 2½" x 42"

From the navy print, cut:
• 6 strips, 2½" x 42"

From the peach print, cut:
• 7 strips, 2½" x 42"

From the dark-gray solid, cut:
• 8 strips, 2½" x 42"
• 2 squares, 15" x 15"; cut in half diagonally to yield 4 half-square triangles

From the orange-and-pink striped print, cut:
• 2½"-wide bias strips, enough to yield 180" of binding strips

Piecing the Star Points

1. Sew together one each of eight different strips, offsetting each strip by approximately 2", to make strip-set A. Press the seam allowances in the direction indicated by the arrow after each strip addition. In a similar manner, make strip-sets B–G.

2"

Strip Set B.
Make 1.

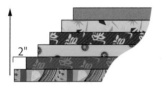

2"

Strip Set C.
Make 1.

2"

Strip Set D.
Make 1.

2"

Strip Set E.
Make 1.

2"

Strip Set F.
Make 1.

2"

Strip Set G.
Make 1.

2. Align the 45°-angle line of your ruler on the raw edge of strip-set A. Trim away and discard the end. Cut eight A segments 2½" wide. Be sure to check the 45° angle after every few cuts, and trim to true up the edge if needed. In a similar manner, cut eight each of segments B–G.

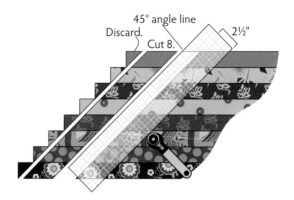

3. Align the 45°-angle line of your ruler on the raw edge of the remaining dark-gray strip. Trim away and discard the end. Cut eight dark-gray 2½"-wide diamonds.

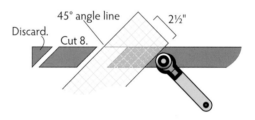

4. To make a star point, sew together one each of segments A–G in the order shown, matching the diamonds at the seam lines. Sew the gray diamond to a G segment. Make eight.

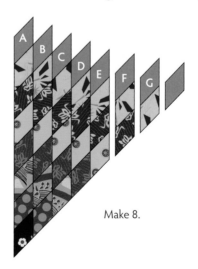

Make 8.

5. Trim the dark-gray points ¼" from the tips of the peach diamonds.

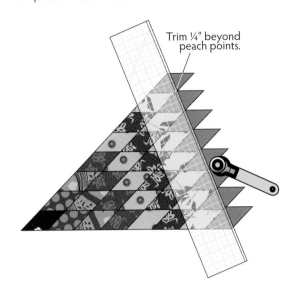

Trim ¼" beyond peach points.

Assembling the Quilt Top

Referring to the assembly diagram, stitch together two star points, matching the diamonds at the seam lines to make a quarter star. Make four. Sew the quarter stars together. Sew 15" half-square triangles to the corners and trim even.

Quilting and Finishing

1. Layer, baste, and quilt. Cindy machine quilted lines ¼" inside each diamond and a meandering flame pattern in the dark-gray areas.
2. Bind the quilt with the orange-and-pink striped 2½"-wide bias strips.

15"

Quilt assembly

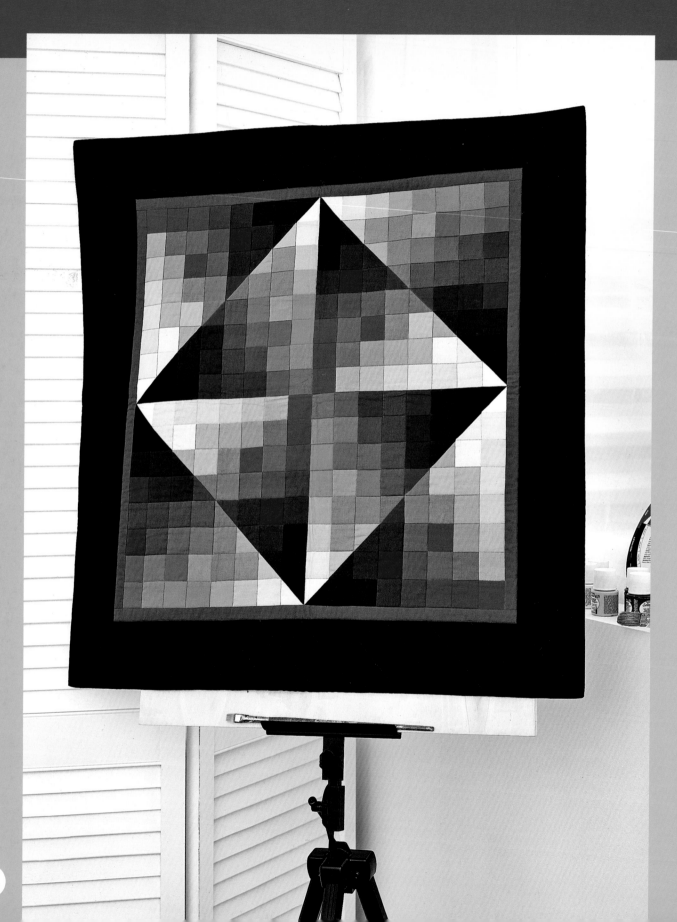

Start with one block, multiply it by four, and then rotate them until you have a piece of artwork that is sheer perfection. With all the fabulous solid fabrics available today, you can make the quilt as shown, or assert your independence and make a color scheme all your own!

Designed by Cindi Edgerton

•

Finished quilt size: 33" x 33"

•

Number of blocks and finished size:
4 Colorwash blocks, 12" x 12"

Planning

This is one of those projects where the thinking takes longer than the sewing! Cindi made the design process simple by laying out one block, and then repeating it for the three remaining blocks.

Materials

Yardage is based on 42"-wide fabric unless noted otherwise.

Navy solid for outer border and binding	1 yard
Teal solid for inner border	¼ yard
72 assorted light, medium, and dark solids for quilt center	6" x 6", *each* piece
Fabric for backing	1¼ yards
Batting	37" x 37"

Cutting

From *each* of the 72 assorted light, medium, and dark solids, cut:
• 4 squares, 2" x 2"

From the teal solid, cut:
• 4 strips, 1¼" x 30"

From the navy solid, cut:
• 4 strips, 4" x 42"
• 4 strips, 2½" x 42"

Piecing the Blocks

1. Using a design wall or other flat surface, arrange light, medium, and dark squares in a shaded arrangement as shown. To plan the light/dark diagonal split across the middle of the block, fold 2" squares in half diagonally and pin in place.

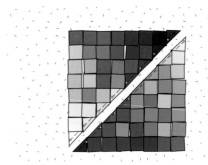

2. When you're satisfied with the color arrangement, remove the folded and pinned squares from the layout, remove the pins, and place the dark and light squares right sides together. Sew along the diagonal; trim, leaving a ¼" seam allowance. Press the pieced squares open, and replace them in the layout.

Make 8 per pieced block.

3. Sew the 2" squares and pieced squares together in eight horizontal rows of eight squares each. Press the seam allowances in opposite directions from row to row. Sew the rows together to make a Colorwash block. Repeat to make a total of four identical blocks.

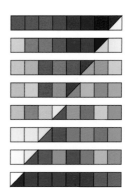 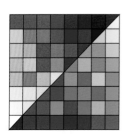

Make 4.

Assembling the Quilt Top

Refer to the assembly diagram for the following steps.

1. Arrange the blocks as shown. Sew the blocks together in two rows of two blocks each. Sew the rows together.

2. Sew teal 1¼" x 30" strips to the sides of the quilt. Trim the ends of the strips even with the top and bottom of the quilt. Sew the remaining teal strips to the top and bottom and trim the ends of the strips even with the sides of the quilt.

3. Sew the navy 4" x 42" strips to the sides of the quilt; trim them even with the top and bottom of the quilt. Sew the remaining navy 4" strips to the top and bottom of the quilt and trim the strips even with the sides of the quilt.

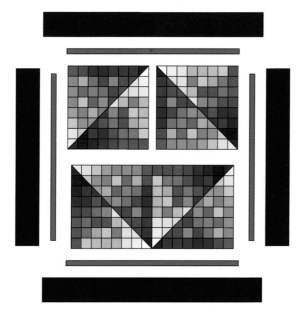

Quilt assembly

Quilting and Finishing

1. Layer and baste the quilt top for the quilting method of your choice (see "Finishing" on page 79). Cindi quilted in the ditch in the quilt center and stitched a simple grid in the outer border.

2. Bind the quilt with the navy 2½"-wide strips.

Apple Blossom Time

Easy piecing is enhanced with fun and relaxing—and portable!—wool-appliqué handwork. A perfect combination for a charming quilt.

Designed by Tammy Tadd; made by Velda Grubbs; machine quilted by Deanna Carls

•

Finished quilt size: 24½" x 24½"

•

Number of blocks and finished size:
1 Card Trick block, 12" x 12"

Planning

Wool appliqué and gingham-covered buttons add delightful dimension to this springtime wall hanging. The wools in yummy colors are from Weeks Dye Works. The appliqué is edged with hand blanket stitch, a relaxing and easy technique.

The appliqué patterns are on page 49, and are printed without seam allowances because you don't need to turn under a seam allowance when using felted wool as the edges won't ravel. Of course, that makes the patterns perfect for fusible cotton appliqués too!

Use an accurate ¼" seam allowance throughout so the pieced border fits well.

Materials

Yardage is based on 42"-wide fabric unless noted otherwise. A fat eighth measures 9" x 20" to 22".

Light-green floral for wide border and pieced border	⅝ yard
Dark-pink dotted and medium-green mottled prints for blocks and pieced border	¼ yard *each*
Light-green mottled and light-pink mottled prints for blocks	7" x 12" piece *each*
White dotted fabric for block background	1 fat eighth
Dark-green felted wool for leaves	10" x 10" piece
Dark-pink felted wool for flowers	10" x 10" piece
Pink felted wool for flowers	8" x 8" piece
Green-and-white gingham for covered buttons and bias binding	¾ yard
Fabric for backing	1 yard
Batting	32" x 32"
Paper-backed fusible web (optional)	½ yard
Embroidery floss in colors to match wool	
Covered-button kit	4 buttons for covering, ⅞" diameter

Cutting

From the white dotted fabric, cut:

- 2 squares, 4⅞" x 4⅞"; cut in half diagonally to make 4 half-square triangles
- 1 square, 5¼" x 5¼"; cut into quarters diagonally to make 4 quarter-square triangles

From *each* of the light-green and light-pink mottled prints, cut:

- 1 square, 4⅞" x 4⅞"; cut in half diagonally to make 2 half-square triangles
- 1 square, 5¼" x 5¼"; cut into quarters diagonally to make 4 quarter-square triangles (2 will be left over)

From the dark-pink dotted fabric, cut:

- 1 square, 4⅞" x 4⅞"; cut in half diagonally to make 2 half-square triangles
- 1 square, 5¼" x 5¼"; cut into quarters diagonally to make 4 quarter-square triangles (2 will be left over)
- 12 squares, 2⅞" x 2⅞"

From the medium-green mottled print, cut:

- 1 square 4⅞" x 4⅞"; cut in half diagonally to make 2 half-square triangles
- 1 square 5¼" x 5¼"; cut into quarters diagonally to make 4 quarter-square triangles (2 will be left over)
- 10 squares, 2⅞" x 2⅞"

From the light-green floral, cut:

- 22 squares, 2⅞" x 2⅞"
- 2 strips, 4½" x 12½"
- 2 strips, 4½" x 20½"

From the green-and-white gingham, cut:

- 2½"-wide bias strips, enough to yield 110" of bias binding
- 4 squares, 1¾" x 1¾" (for covered buttons)

From the dark-green wool, cut:

- 12 of A

From the dark-pink wool, cut:

- 4 of B

From the pink wool, cut:

- 4 of C

Making the Card Trick Block

1. Stitch the white quarter-square triangles to light-pink, medium-pink, light-green, and medium-green quarter-square triangles. Make one of each color combination, making sure the white triangle is always on the left, as shown.

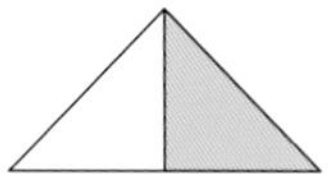

2. In the same manner, sew a dark-pink and a light-green quarter-square triangle together as shown. Repeat to join a light-pink and medium-green quarter-square triangle.

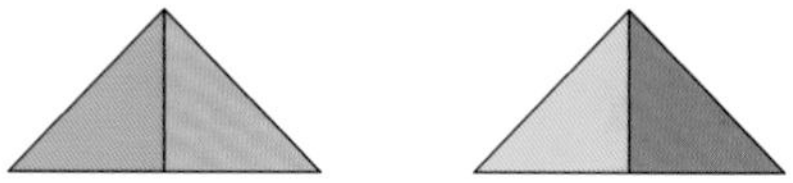

Make 1 of each.

3. Lay out the pieced triangle units from steps 1 and 2 with the half-square triangles as shown. Sew the pieced triangles to the larger half-square triangles first and place them back in the layout. Then sew the half-square triangle pairs together. Once all the triangles have been pieced into squares, sew them together in rows and join the rows to complete one Card Trick block.

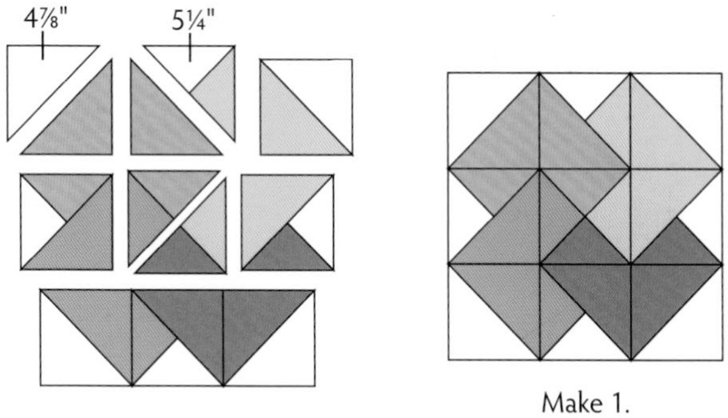

Make 1.

Making the Pieced Border

1. Draw a diagonal line on the wrong side of the light-green floral 2⅞" squares. Place a marked square on a dark-pink dotted 2⅞" square, right sides together. Sew ¼" from each side of the marked line. Cut the squares apart on the marked line and press them open to make pieced squares. Make 24. In the same manner, use light-green floral and medium-green mottled 2⅞" squares to make 20 pieced squares.

Make 24.   Make 20.

2. For a side border, stitch together six light-green floral/dark-pink dotted pieced squares and four light-green floral/medium-green mottled pieced squares, watching positioning and orientation. Make two.

   For the top and bottom border, sew together six each of the light-green floral/ medium-green mottled pieced squares and light-green floral/dark-pink dotted pieced squares, watching orientation and positioning.

Side borders.
Make 2.

Top and Bottom borders.
Make 2.

Assembling the Quilt Top

1. Sew light-green floral 12½"-long strips to the sides of the Card Trick block. Stitch light-green floral 20½"-long strips to the top and bottom. Press the seam allowances toward the green strips.

2. Sew the shorter pieced border strips to the sides of the quilt top, making sure the center pink triangles point away from the quilt center. Sew the longer pieced borders to the top and bottom of the quilt in the same manner. Press all seam allowances toward the wide green borders.

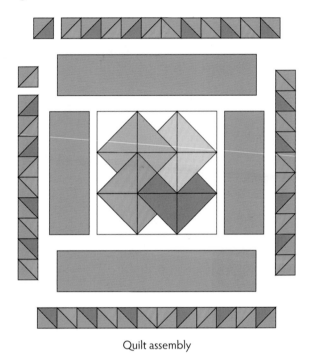

Quilt assembly

Appliquéing the Quilt Top

Hold the pieces in place temporarily by simply pinning or basting them in place.

1. Using two strands of matching embroidery floss, hand blanket stitch around the appliqués. Machine blanket stitch may be used if you prefer.

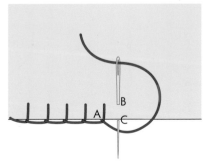

Blanket stitch

2. Following the manufacturer's instructions, use the gingham 1¾" squares to cover the buttons. Stitch the buttons to the flower centers.

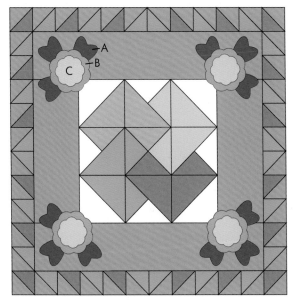

Quilting and Finishing

1. Layer, baste, and quilt. Deanna machine quilted partial flowers in the block, one in each color group. She outline quilted the white patches in the Card Trick block, appliquéd flowers, and outer-border triangles, and used detail quilting to fill the background of the inner border.
2. Bind the quilt with the green-and-white gingham 2½"-wide bias strips.

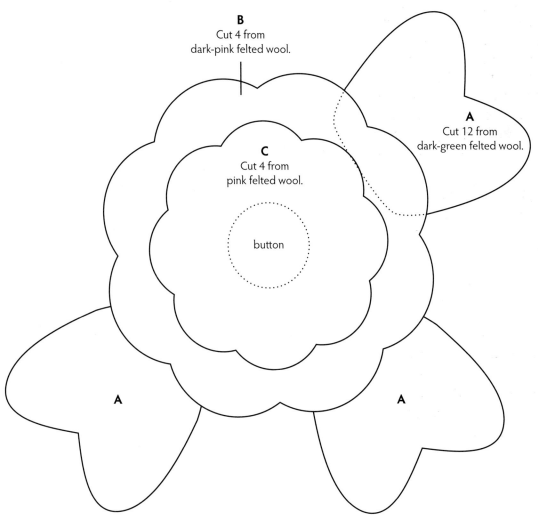

B
Cut 4 from
dark-pink felted wool.

A
Cut 12 from
dark-green felted wool.

C
Cut 4 from
pink felted wool.

button

A

A

Black, White, and Red All Around

Crisp prints in black and white are the focus of this striking quilt. If black and white isn't your favorite combination, you can simply substitute another pair of dark and light colors and add an accent color for the narrow inner border to make this project truly your own.

Designed by Kathie Holland; machine quilted by Lorre Fleming

•

Finished quilt size: 65" x 65"

Planning

The graphic appeal of Kathie's design demonstrates the importance of line and texture in planning an effective quilt pattern. This quilt is simply made of squares and half-square-triangle units, so laying out the pieces on a design wall or other flat surface before sewing will easily enable you to visualize the overall design and to move pieces around until you're happy with the placement of each piece.

Materials

Yardage is based on 42"-wide fabric unless noted otherwise.

Black-and-white vine print for outer border and binding	2¼ yards
Assorted white-with-black prints	1¾ yards *total*
Assorted black-with-white prints	1¾ yards *total*
Red tone-on-tone print for corners and inner border	⅝ yard
Fabric for backing	4¼ yards
Batting	69" x 69"

Cutting

From the assorted white-with-black prints, cut a total of:
• 18 squares, 6⅞" x 6⅞"
• 12 squares, 6½" x 6½"

From the red tone-on-tone print, cut:
• 6 strips, 1¾" x 42"
• 2 squares, 6⅞" x 6⅞"

From the assorted black-with-white prints, cut:
• 16 squares, 6⅞" x 6⅞"
• 16 squares, 6½" x 6½"

From the black-and-white vine print, cut:
• 2 strips, 7½" x 55", cut on *lengthwise grain**
• 2 strips, 7½" x 69", cut on *lengthwise grain**
• 7 strips, 2½" x 42"

*Cut first.

Making the Quilt

1. On wrong side of a white 6⅞" square, draw a diagonal line with the marking tool of your choice. Place the white square on a red 6⅞" square, right sides together. Sew ¼" from each side of the marked line; cut apart on the marked line. Press open to make two pieced squares. Repeat to make a total of four red-and-white pieced squares. In the same manner, use 16 white and 16 black 6⅞" squares to make a total of 32 black-and-white pieced squares.

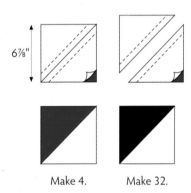

Make 4.   Make 32.

2. Referring to the assembly diagram, arrange and sew eight rows of eight squares each, using pieced squares and assorted white and black 6½" squares. Sew the rows together.
3. Stitch the red 1¾"-wide strips together end to end. From this long strip, cut four strips, 55" long. Sew a red strip to each side of the quilt; trim the strips even with the top and bottom. Stitch the remaining red strips to the top and bottom; trim the strips even with the sides.
4. Sew the black 55"-long strips to the sides of the quilt; trim the strips even. Sew the remaining strips to the top and bottom; trim the strips even.

Quilting and Finishing

1. Layer, baste, and quilt. Lorre machine quilted a continuous swirl pattern in the white areas, and followed the star angles with repeating lines of quilting in the black areas. She quilted the red border and corner triangles in straight lines and filled the outer border with a large feathered vine.
2. Bind the quilt with the black-and-white vine-print 2½"-wide strips.

Assembly diagram

Black, White, and Red All Around

Daisy Power

Even when the calendar says we're still in the grip of winter, there's no reason you can't think spring! Put a little spring into your sewing with this wall quilt that's quick to piece and to appliqué with the help of fusible web.

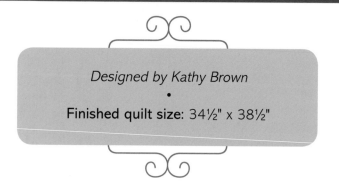

Designed by Kathy Brown

•

Finished quilt size: 34½" x 38½"

Planning

We give you patterns for one large and one small flower, but Kathy cut and arranged each flower slightly differently. She also fussy cut her flower centers (pattern C) to feature a printed swirl motif. Do likewise if you wish.

Materials

Yardage is based on 42"-wide fabric unless noted otherwise.

Multicolored plaid for vase, fourth border, and bias binding	1¼ yards
Assorted bright polka-dot and swirl prints for flowers and pieced border	¾ yard *total*
White-on-white print for appliqué background	⅝ yard
Aqua print for first and third borders	½ yard
Fabric for backing	1⅜ yards
Batting	38" x 42"
Paper-backed fusible web	1 yard
⅛"-wide green ribbon	1⅜ yards

Cutting

Appliqué patterns are on pages 56–57; they've been reversed for fusible appliqué.

From the assorted bright polka-dot and swirl prints, cut:
• 24 rectangles, 2½" x 4½"
• 4 matching sets of:
  3 of A
  3 of B
• 4 matching sets of:
  1 of D
  4 of E
  8 of C

From the multicolored plaid, cut:
• 4 strips, 4½" x 42"*
• 2½"-wide bias strip, enough to yield 158" of bias binding*
• 1 F vase

From the white-on-white print:
• 1 rectangle 18½" x 22½"

From the aqua print:
• 8 strips 1½" x 42"

Cut first.

Appliquéing the Quilt Center

Refer to the placement diagram for positioning the ribbon stems and appliqué pieces.

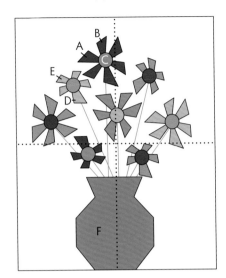

Placement diagram

1. Trace patterns A–F onto the paper side of paper-backed fusible web. Cut the patterns apart, leaving ¼" beyond the drawn lines. Following the manufacturer's instructions, fuse the patterns to the wrong side of the appropriate fabrics. Cut out each shape on the drawn lines.

2. For flower stems, cut the green ribbon into the following lengths: 6¼", 2¼", 9¾", 7¼", 5¼", 8¾", 2", 5½". These ribbon stems will be positioned from left to right at the vase opening.

3. Finger-press the white rectangle in half vertically and horizontally; use the folds as a placement guide. Referring to the placement diagram above, position the stems. Using a wide zigzag stitch and green thread, stitch over the ribbon strips to hold them in place.

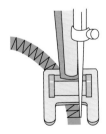

4. Following the manufacturer's instructions, position and fuse the petals, leaves, flower centers, and vase in place. Using a narrow zigzag stitch, stitch around the appliqué shapes to secure them.

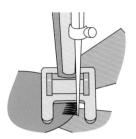

Assembling the Quilt

1. Referring to the assembly diagram on page 56, sew aqua 1½"-wide strips to sides of the appliquéd quilt center; trim the strips even with the top and bottom of the quilt center. Stitch aqua strips to the top and bottom of the quilt center; trim the strips even with sides.

2. Sew six assorted bright 2½" x 4½" rectangles together, end to end. Make four pieced strips. Sew a strip to each side of the quilt top; then sew the remaining pieced strips to the top and bottom.

Make 4.

3. Sew aqua 1½"-wide strips to the sides of the quilt top; trim them even with the top and bottom of the quilt. Stitch the remaining aqua strips to the top and bottom of the quilt; trim them even with the sides.

4. Sew the multicolored plaid 4½"-wide strips to the quilt top in the same manner.

Assembly diagram

Quilting and Finishing

1. Layer, baste, and quilt. Kathy machine quilted a meandering pattern on the background, vase, and outer border. She quilted in the ditch around the aqua borders and stitched a large X on each rectangle in the pieced border.
2. Bind the quilt with the multicolored plaid 2½"-wide bias strips.

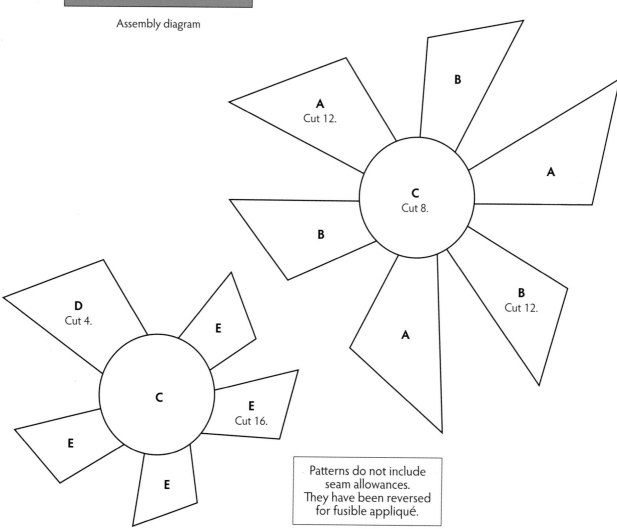

A
Cut 12.

B

A

C
Cut 8.

B

B
Cut 12.

A

D
Cut 4.

E

C

E

E
Cut 16.

E

E

Patterns do not include seam allowances. They have been reversed for fusible appliqué.

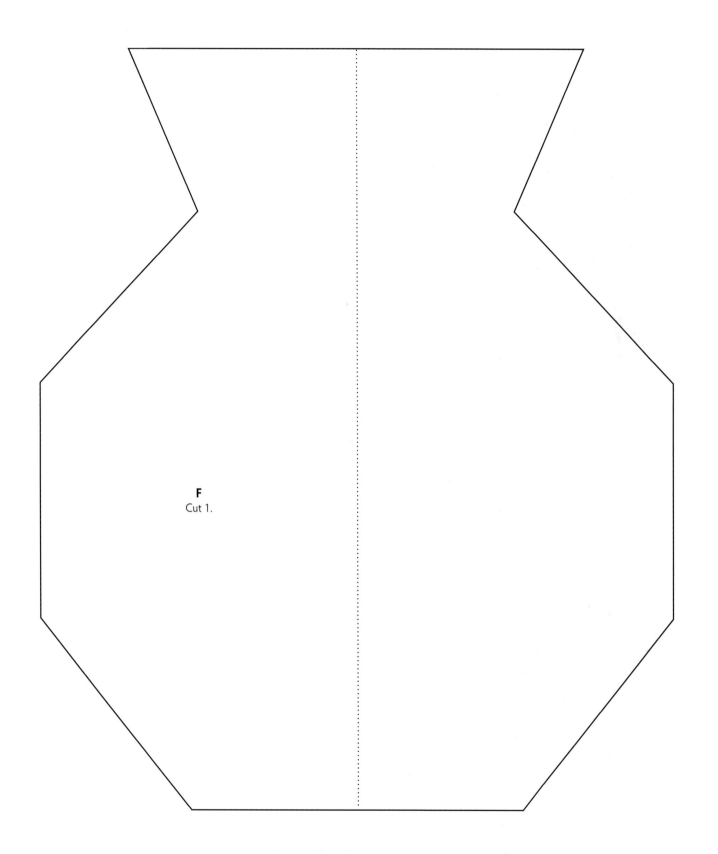

F
Cut 1.

Tulip Parade

Well known for her use of batiks, quilt artist Joyce Robinson has skillfully taken pieces of her favorite type of fabric and turned them into a stunning, contemporary work of art. Placed on a black background, the border flowers burst with a vitality that only the tulip fields in Holland could rival.

Designed by Joyce Robinson

•

Finished quilt size: 52" x 52"

Planning

Follow our quick instructions to create your own pleasing tulip display. The flowers are fused in place on the black border, and they're sewn and quilted at the same time. Notice that each of Joyce's tulips and leaves is a slightly different shape. We provide you with three tulip flowers and three pairs of leaves to get you started, but be sure to vary the flower and leaf shapes when cutting them out.

Joyce used Clover fusible bias tape for the stems; if you can't find that, you can substitute ribbon for the stems. Be sure to vary the length of each stem from flower to flower, just as you would find flowers in nature.

Materials

Assorted light, medium, dark, and bright batiks for squares, flowers, leaves, and pieced binding	3 yards *total* (or 20 fat quarters)
Black solid for appliquéd border	1⅝ yards
Fabric for backing	3⅜ yards
Batting	56" x 56"
Paper-backed fusible web	3 yards
Purple ¼"-wide fusible bias tape *or* ¼"-wide ribbon	11 yards

Cutting

The appliqué patterns, opposite, have been reversed for fusible appliqué.

From the assorted batiks, cut:
- 5 squares from *each*, 3¾" x 3¾" (100 total)
- 40 flowers
- 40 matching pairs of leaves
- Enough strips, 2½" x 3" to 6", to make 220" of binding when sewn together

From the black solid, cut:
- 4 strips 10" x 56", cut on *lengthwise grain*

Assembling the Quilt Top

Refer to the assembly diagram below for the following steps.

1. Arrange 10 rows of 10 assorted batik squares on your design wall or other flat surface. When you're satisfied with the color placement, sew the rows together to complete the quilt center.
2. Sew a black solid 10" x 56" strip to each side of the quilt top, starting and stopping ¼" from corners. Miter the corners, referring to "Borders with Mitered Corners" on page 78.

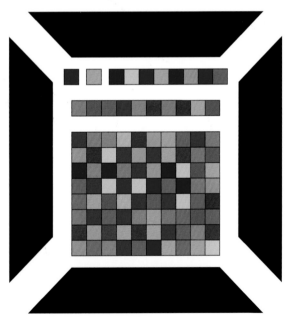

Assembly diagram

Adding the Appliqué

1. Trace the tulips and leaves onto the paper side of paper-backed fusible web. Cut the pieces apart, leaving a ¼" margin beyond the drawn lines. Following the manufacturer's instructions, fuse the shapes to the wrong side of the desired fabrics, and then cut out the tulips and leaves on the drawn lines.
2. Press the quilt top in half lengthwise and crosswise; use the folds as a placement guide. Referring to the quilt photo (page 58), center a prepared tulip, pair of leaves, and purple fusible bias-tape stem (cut 4" to 6" in length) on the black border along the fold line. Align the stem bottom with the raw edge of the border. Arrange four tulips (varying flower and leaf fabrics and stem length) on each side of the center tulip. When you're satisfied with the arrangement, fuse the flowers, leaves, and stems in place. Repeat the process on the three remaining borders.
3. In the same manner, cover each mitered corner seam with a flower, stem, and leaves.

Quilting and Finishing

1. Layer and baste the quilt top for the quilting method of your choice (see "Finishing" on page 79). Using rose thread and free-motion machine quilting, Joyce added a meandering pattern on the center squares and covered each flower and leaf with a design that roughly follows their shapes. Stitching lines cross, and no lines are spaced evenly, adding a natural dimensional feel to the piece. She used a wide free-motion zigzag and purple thread to secure the stems. She filled the border background with a tight meandering pattern in black thread.
2. To make the pieced binding, sew the assorted batik 2½" x 3" to 6" strips (varying color from section to section) end to end to make a binding strip that's 220" long. Use the strip to bind your quilt.

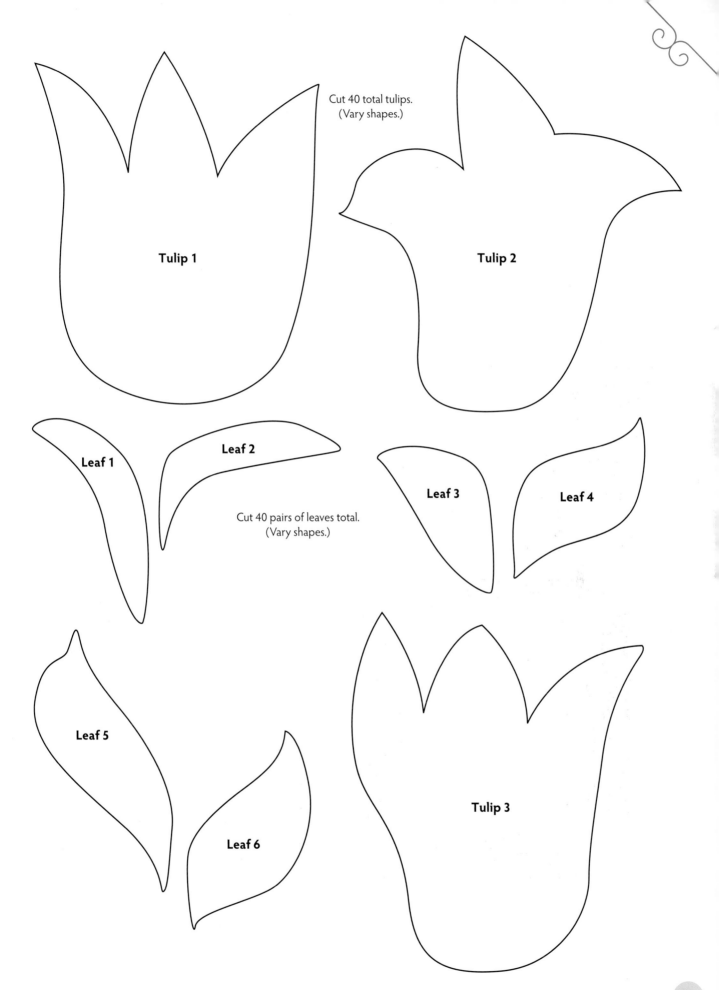

Cut 40 total tulips.
(Vary shapes.)

Tulip 1

Tulip 2

Leaf 1

Leaf 2

Cut 40 pairs of leaves total.
(Vary shapes.)

Leaf 3

Leaf 4

Leaf 5

Leaf 6

Tulip 3

Yuletide Classic

Create antique appeal with today's techniques. This timeless pattern will grace your wall in no time at all when you use machine appliqué. Of course, you can sit back and relax and appliqué by hand if you like!

Designed by Kathie Holland

•

Finished quilt size: 60½" x 60½"

•

Number of blocks and finished size:
4 Yuletide Classic blocks, 24" x 24"
8 Nine-Patch blocks, 6" x 6"

Materials

Yardage is based on 42"-wide fabric unless noted otherwise.

Tan-on-tan print for appliqué background and pieced border	3 yards
Green print for leaves, flowers, and Nine Patch blocks	2¾ yards
Red tone-on-tone print for flowers, Nine Patch blocks, and border	1¾ yards
Red small-scale print for flowers and binding	1 yard
Fabric for backing	3⅞ yards
Batting	65" x 65"

Planning

This striking wall hanging is a great project for practicing the appliqué method of your choice. When placing appliqué pieces, keep in mind that background squares are appliquéd first, and then squared up and trimmed to 24½" x 24½". Kathie machine appliquéd using color-coordinated threads for blanket stitching. If you prefer, you can use any other appliqué method, including hand appliqué and fusible appliqué.

Cutting

Appliqué patterns are on pages 66 and 67 and do not include seam allowances. For more on cutting and preparing appliqué pieces, see "Appliqué" on page 75.

From the tan-on-tan print, cut:
- 4 squares, 26" x 26"*
- 8 strips, 2½" x 24", cut on *lengthwise grain*

From the red tone-on-tone print, cut:
- 1 strip, 2½" x 44", cut on *lengthwise grain**
- 18 strips 2½" x 24", cut on *lengthwise grain**
- 16 *each* of A and B
- 5 of G

From the green print, cut:
- 2 strips, 2½" x 44", cut on *lengthwise grain**
- 1 strip, 2½" x 24", cut on *lengthwise grain**
- 16 of D*
- 16 of C
- 5 of F

From the red small-scale print, cut:
- 7 strips, 2½" x 42"
- 5 of flower E

*Cut first.

Appliquéing the Blocks

1. Finger-press the tan 26" squares in half vertically, horizontally, and along both diagonals.
2. Using the folds as placement guides, position the appliqués in alphabetical order, keeping in mind that the square will be trimmed to 24½" x 24½" (finished block size is 24" square). Using your appliqué method of choice, appliqué in place. Make four blocks.

3. Trim the blocks to 24½" square.

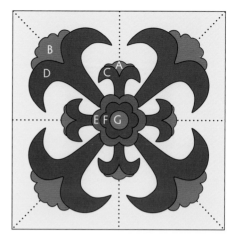

Make 4.

Piecing the Border Units

1. Sew one tan and two red 2½" x 24" strips together. Repeat to make eight of these strip sets. Press the seam allowances toward the red strips, and then cut a 21½" length from each strip set.

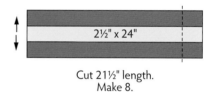

Cut 21½" length.
Make 8.

2. Stitch a strip set using two green and one red 2½" x 44" strip as shown. Sew a strip set using two red and one green 2½" x 24" strip. Press all seam allowances toward the green strips. Cut 16 segments 2½" wide from the 44" strip set, and 8 segments 2½" wide from the 24" strip set.

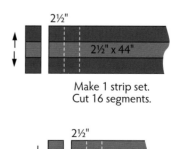

Make 1 strip set.
Cut 16 segments.

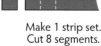

Make 1 strip set.
Cut 8 segments.

3. Sew the strip segments together as shown to make a Nine Patch block. Make eight total.

Make 8.

Assembling the Quilt Top

Refer to the assembly diagram below and photo on page 62 for the following steps.

1. Sew the appliquéd blocks together in two rows of two blocks each for the quilt center.
2. Appliqué the remaining E–G appliqués to the center of the quilt, referring to the photo for placement.
3. Sew together two 21½"-long segments and one Nine Patch block. Make two side-border strips and sew them to the sides of the quilt. Sew together two 21½"-long segments and three Nine Patch blocks. Make two and sew them to the top and bottom of the quilt.

Quilting and Finishing

1. Layer and baste the quilt top, batting, and backing for the quilting method of your choice (see "Finishing" on page 79). Kathie outline quilted the appliqué pieces by machine, and added dimension to the leaves and flowers by echo quilting inside the shapes. She filled the background with a meandering pattern, and quilted the border strips with a trailing leaf pattern. She used diagonal lines to form an X on each Nine Patch block.
2. Bind the quilt with the red 2½"-wide strips.

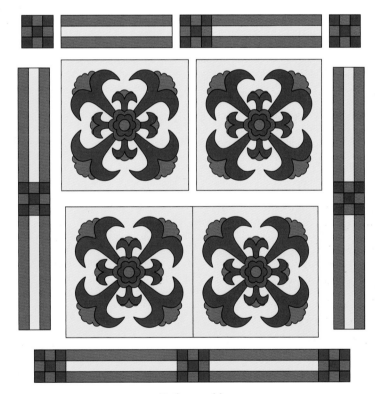

Quilt assembly

B
Cut 16.

A
Cut 16.

E
Cut 5.

F
Cut 5.

G
Cut 5.

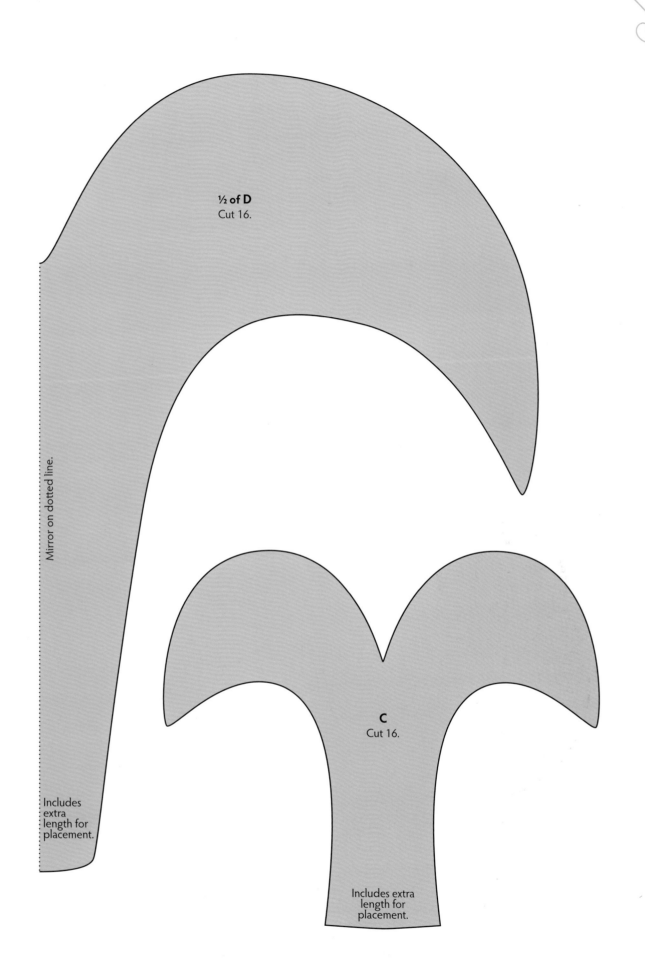

½ **of D**
Cut 16.

Mirror on dotted line.

Includes
extra
length for
placement.

C
Cut 16.

Includes extra
length for
placement.

A Thoroughly Modern Mary

Jan Carlson, cofounder and former president of the Baltimore Appliqué Society, challenged herself and friend Pat Sloan to create a modern project using a block design from Mary Mannakee's famous Baltimore album quilt. Can you spy the block in this historic quilt that served as the starting point for this challenge?

Modern version of a classic Baltimore album quilt, made by Jan Carlson

•

Finished quilt size: 27½" x 27½"

•

Number of blocks and finished size:
1 Mary Mannakee block, 16" x 16"

Since its arrival at the Daughters of the American Revolution Museum in 1945, the original Mary Mannakee quilt, made circa 1850, has been restored, patterned, and copied many times. Mary's legacy lives on, in every new project sparked by her Baltimore album classic.

Planning

The instructions are for Jan's bright version, shown on page 68. Pat's quilt is shown here. She pieced her Four-Patch appliqué background from two 9" squares each of two different light-brown prints, and then appliquéd using a machine blanket stitch and trimmed the quilt center to 16½" square before adding the borders and border appliqué. Pat also cut a circle for the center of the appliqué from a contrasting fabric, instead of trimming it away to expose the background as Jan did. Feel free to play with design decisions like these when you work on your own version.

Materials

Yardage is based on 42"-wide fabric unless noted otherwise.

Green-and-black striped fabric for vines (E, G, G reverse)	⅞ yard
Red-and-orange mottled print for appliqué background and berries (H, I)	⅝ yard
Black solid for outer border	⅝ yard
Green-and-black medium-scale polka-dot fabric for inner border and binding	½ yard
Green checked fabric for leaves and berry caps (D, J)	¼ yard
Blue striped fabric for flowers (A)	9" x 14" piece
Green-and-black large-scale polka-dot fabric for flower bases (C)	9" x 9" piece
Black polka-dot fabric for appliqué center (F)	9" x 9" piece
Orange small-scale print for flower centers (B)	5" x 7" piece
Blue mottled print for berries (H)	5" x 5" piece
Fabric for backing	1 yard
Batting	32" x 32"

Cutting

Appliqué patterns are on pages 72–74 and do not include seam allowances. For more on cutting and preparing appliqué pieces, see "Appliqué" on page 75.

From the black solid, cut:
• 2 strips, 5½" x 32"
• 2 strips, 5½" x 20"

From the green-and-black medium-scale polka-dot fabric, cut:
• 4 strips, 1" x 20"
• 4 strips, 2½" x 42"

From the red-and-orange mottled fabric, cut:
• 1 square, 18" x 18"*
• 24 of H
• 12 of I

From the blue striped fabric, cut:
• 4 of A

From the orange small-scale print, cut:
• 4 of B

From the green-and-black large-scale polka-dot fabric, cut:
• 4 of C

From the green checked fabric, cut:
• 32 of D
• 12 of J

From the green-and-black striped fabric, cut:
• 4 of E
• 2 *each*, G and G reverse vines

From the black polka-dot fabric, cut:
• 1 of F

From the blue mottled print, cut:
• 8 of H

*Cut first.

Appliquéing the Block

1. Finger-press the red-and-orange mottled 18" square in half vertically and horizontally and along both diagonals.
2. Using the folds as placement guides, position pieces A–F in alphabetical order onto the background. Using the appliqué method of your choice, appliqué the pieces in place.
3. Trim the completed appliquéd square to 16½" square.

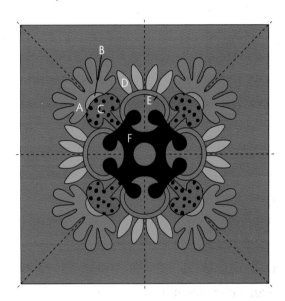

Assembling the Quilt Top and Appliquéing the Border

1. Referring to the assembly diagram on page 72, stitch green-and-black polka-dot 1" x 20" strips to the sides of the block; trim the strips even with the top and bottom of the block. Stitch the remaining two green-and-black polka-dot 1"-wide strips to the top and bottom of the quilt top and trim the strips even.
2. Sew black solid 5½" x 20" strips to the quilt sides; trim the strips even with the quilt top. Sew the remaining black solid 5½"-wide strips to the top and bottom of the quilt and trim the strips even.

3. Referring to the photo on page 68, position appliqués G–J and the remaining D leaves onto the outer border. Appliqué the pieces in place.

Quilting and Finishing

1. Layer, baste, and quilt. Jan hand quilted around the appliqués, and then filled the background with straight lines spaced ½" apart, radiating from the quilt center.
2. Bind the quilt with the green-and-black polka-dot 2½"-wide strips.

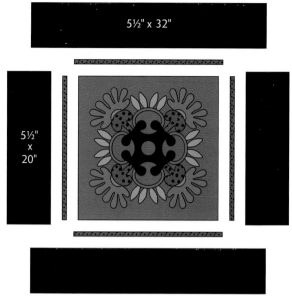

Assembly diagram

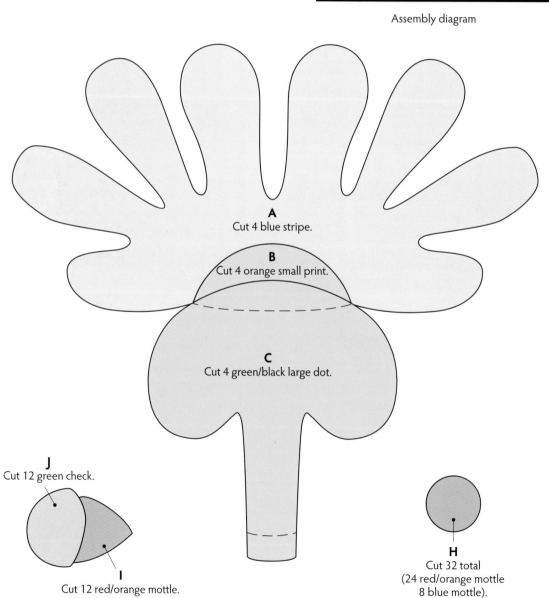

A
Cut 4 blue stripe.

B
Cut 4 orange small print.

C
Cut 4 green/black large dot.

J
Cut 12 green check.

I
Cut 12 red/orange mottle.

H
Cut 32 total
(24 red/orange mottle
8 blue mottle).

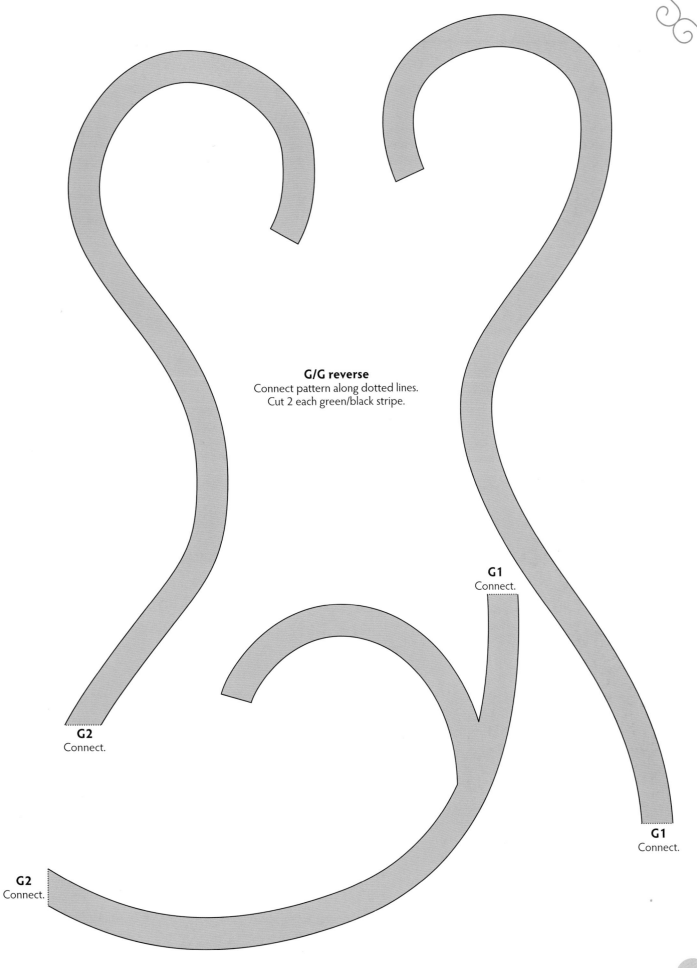

G/G reverse
Connect pattern along dotted lines.
Cut 2 each green/black stripe.

G1
Connect.

G2
Connect.

G1
Connect.

G2
Connect.

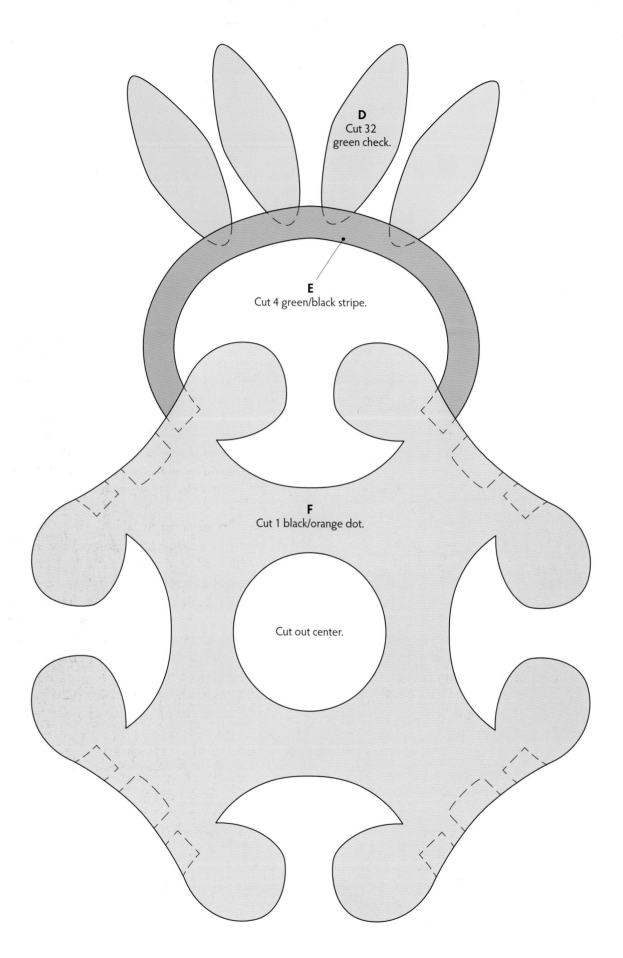

D
Cut 32
green check.

E
Cut 4 green/black stripe.

F
Cut 1 black/orange dot.

Cut out center.

Quiltmaking Basics

If you're new to quilting or just need a refresher, the following techniques will help you create the quilts in this book.

Machine Piecing

The most important thing to remember about machine piecing is to maintain a consistent ¼"-wide seam allowance. This is necessary for the seams to match and for the resulting block or quilt to measure the desired finished size. Measurements for all components of each quilt are based on blocks that finish accurately to the desired size plus ¼" on each edge for seam allowances.

Seam Allowance

Take the time to establish an exact ¼"-wide seam-allowance guide on your machine. Some machines have a special quilting foot that measures exactly ¼" from the center needle position to the edge of the foot. If your machine doesn't have such a foot, create a seam guide by placing the edge of a piece of tape or moleskin ¼" away from the needle.

Chain Piecing

Chain piecing saves time and thread. It's helpful when you're sewing many identical units. Simply sew the first pair of pieces from cut edge to cut edge. At the end of the seam, stop sewing, but don't cut the thread. Feed the next pair of pieces under the presser foot, as close as possible to the first pair. Continue sewing without cutting the threads. When all the pieces are sewn, remove the chain from the machine, clip the threads, and press.

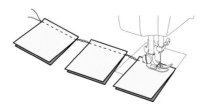

Appliqué

There are many techniques for appliqué and there's not space to cover all of them here. For additional information on other methods or more details, consult some of the many excellent books on the topic, or visit your local quilt shop to look into classes.

The first step for any method of appliqué is to make a template either from plastic or from freezer paper. Plastic templates are more durable, and if one shape is repeated many times in the quilt, some quilters make a plastic template, which is then used to draw multiple freezer-paper templates or even multiple shapes on fusible web. Freezer-paper templates will temporarily adhere to the fabric if the shiny side is placed face down on the fabric and pressed. You can reuse freezer-paper templates a few times before they will no longer stick to the fabric.

Basted-Edge Preparation

In this method, the edges of appliqué pieces are turned under and secured with a basting stitch before appliquéing by hand or machine.

1. Trace the appliqué pattern onto the dull side of freezer paper. Trace the pattern in reverse if it's asymmetrical and has not already been reversed for tracing. Symmetrical patterns don't need to be reversed.
2. Cut the freezer-paper template on the drawn lines and press it to the wrong side of the appliqué fabric.
3. Cut out the fabric shapes, adding a scant ¼" seam allowance around each shape.

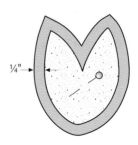

4. Turn the seam allowance over the edge of the paper and baste, close to the edge and through the paper. Clip the corners and baste the inner curves first. On outer curves, take small running stitches through the fabric only to ease in the fullness. Do not turn under edges that will be covered by another piece.

5. For sharp points, first fold the corner to the inside; then fold the remaining seam allowance over the paper.

Fold corners to inside.　　Fold remaining seam allowances over paper.

6. When all seam allowances are turned and basted, press the appliqués.

7. Pin and then stitch the pieces to the background by machine (see "Machine Appliqué" on page 77) or by hand with the traditional hand-appliqué stitch, right.

8. After stitching, remove the basting stitches, carefully slit the background fabric behind the appliqué shape, and pull out the paper. Use tweezers if necessary to loosen the freezer paper.

Needle-Turn Hand Appliqué

With this technique, the edge of each piece is turned under with the edge of your needle as you stitch it to the background. Use a longer needle, such as a Sharp or milliner's, to help you control the seam allowance and turn it under as you stitch.

1. Place the template right side up on the right side of the fabric and trace around it with a No. 2 pencil or a white pencil, depending on your fabric color and print.

2. Cut out the shape, adding a scant ¼" seam allowance all around.

3. Pin or baste the appliqué piece in position on the background fabric.

4. Beginning on a straight edge, bring your needle up through the background and the appliqué piece, just inside the drawn line. Use the tip of the needle to gently turn under the seam allowance, about ½" at a time. Hold the turned seam allowance firmly between thethumb and first finger of one hand as you stitch the appliqué to the background fabric with your other hand. Use the traditional hand-appliqué stitch described below.

Traditional Hand-Appliqué Stitch

1. Thread a needle with a single strand of thread and knot one end. Use a thread color that matches the appliqué piece.

2. Slip the needle into the seam allowance from the wrong side of the appliqué, bringing it out on the fold line. Start the first stitch by inserting the needle into the background fabric right next to the folded edge of the appliqué where the thread exits the appliqué shape.

3. Let the needle travel under the background fabric, parallel to the edge of the appliqué; bring the needle up about ⅛" away through the edge of the appliqué, catching only one or two threads of the folded edge. Insert the needle into the background fabric right next to the folded edge. Let the needle travel under the background, and again bring it up about ⅛" away, catching just the edge of the appliqué. Give the thread a slight tug and continue stitching.

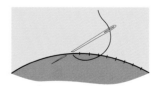

Appliqué stitch

4. Stitch around the appliqué, taking a couple of stitches beyond where you started. Knot the thread on the wrong side of the background fabric, behind the appliqué.

Bias Vines

Vines are narrow and curved, so it's best to cut them on the bias—at a 45° angle to the selvedge edge. The width to cut the strips is given in the project instructions.

1. Fold the bias strips in half lengthwise, wrong sides together. Stitch ¼" from the raw edge and trim the seam allowance to ⅛".
2. Press the tube flat, centering the seam allowance on the back so the raw edge isn't visible from the front. Using a bias bar makes pressing faster and easier.

Bias bar

Machine Appliqué

For the least visible stitches, use monofilament—clear for light-colored appliqués or smoke for medium or dark colors—and a narrow zigzag stitch. If you want your stitches to show as a more decorative element, use a matching or contrasting-color thread in the top of your machine. Use a neutral-color thread to match your background fabric in the bobbin.

1. Set your machine for a narrow zigzag stitch (about ⅛" or 4mm wide) and do a practice sample to test your stitches and tension. An open-toe presser foot is helpful for machine appliqué.
2. Prepare each appliqué piece using the basted-edge preparation method on page 75. Pin the pieces to the background and begin stitching the pieces that are not overlapped by any other pieces.
3. Begin stitching with the needle just outside the appliqué piece and take two or three straight stitches in place to lock the thread. Make sure the needle is on the right of the appliqué and that the zigzag stitches will go into the appliqué piece. (You can use any decorative stitch on your machine.)

4. Stitch curved shapes slowly to maintain control, stopping and pivoting as needed.

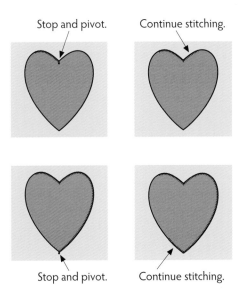

Stop and pivot.   Continue stitching.

Stop and pivot.   Continue stitching.

5. Stitch completely around the appliqué until you're slightly beyond the starting point. Take two or three straight stitches in place to lock the threads; clip the thread tails.
6. To remove the freezer paper, carefully trim away the background fabric behind the appliqué, leaving a generous ¼" seam allowance to keep your appliqué secure. Use tweezers as needed. (Bias stems and vines and fused appliqué shapes will not have paper to remove, so it's not necessary to cut away the background.)

 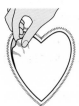

Fusible Appliqué

This appliqué method is fast and easy. Many fusible products are available for applying one piece of fabric to another, but fabrics do stiffen after application, so choose a lightweight fusible web. Follow the manufacturer's instructions for the product you select. Unless the patterns are symmetrical or the pattern has already been reversed, you'll need to reverse the templates when you draw them on the paper side of the fusible web. Do not add seam allowances to the appliqué pieces, but leave a ¼" to ½" cutting margin around each shape drawn on the fusible appliqué. For large appliqués, you can cut out the center of the fusible web, leaving a "donut" of web so that the centers of your appliqués will remain soft and unfused.

For quilts that will be washed often, finish the edges of the appliqués by stitching around them with a decorative stitch, such as a blanket stitch (by hand or machine) or zigzag stitch.

Borders

For best results, measure the quilt top before cutting and sewing the border strips to the quilt. Measure the quilt top through the center in both directions to determine how long to cut the border strips. This step ensures that the finished quilt will be as straight and as square as possible, without wavy edges.

Plain Borders

Many of these quilts call for plain border strips. Some of these strips are cut along the crosswise grain and joined where extra length is needed. Others are cut lengthwise and do not need to be pieced.

1. Measure the length of the quilt top through the center. Cut two borders to this measurement. Determine the midpoints of the border and quilt top by folding them in half and creasing or pinning the centers. Then pin the borders to opposite sides of the quilt top,

matching the center marks and ends and easing as necessary. Sew the border strips in place. Press the seam allowances toward the borders.

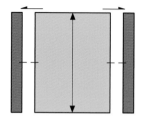

Measure center of quilt,
top to bottom. Mark centers.

2. Measure the width of the quilt top through the center, including the side borders just added. Cut two borders to this measurement. Mark the centers of the quilt edges and the border strips. Pin the borders to the top and bottom edges of the quilt top, matching the center marks and ends and easing as necessary. Sew the border strips in place. Press the seam allowances toward the borders.

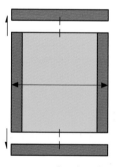

Measure center of quilt, side to side,
including border strips. Mark centers.

Borders with Mitered Corners

1. Starting and stopping ¼" from the quilt corners and backstitching to secure, sew the border strips to the quilt top. Press the seam allowances toward the quilt center.
2. Fold the quilt on the diagonal at one corner, right sides together. Align the border-strip raw edges and border seams at the ¼" backstitched point; pin together.

3. Align a ruler edge with the fold, extending the ruler completely across the border. Draw a line from the backstitched point to the border raw edges. Stitch along the drawn line, backstitching at both ends. Press the seam allowances open.

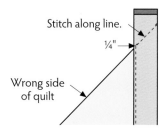

Stitch along line.

¼"

Wrong side of quilt

4. With the quilt right side up, align the 45°-angle line of the ruler on the seam line to check the accuracy. If the corner is flat and square, trim the excess fabric to a ¼" seam allowance. Repeat for all corners.

45°

Right side of quilt

Finishing

The quilt sandwich consists of backing, batting, and the quilt top. Cut the quilt backing 4" to 6" longer and wider than the quilt top. Baste the layers together with thread for hand quilting or safety pins for machine quilting. Quilt by hand or machine.

Hand Quilting

To quilt by hand, you'll need short, sturdy needles (called Betweens), quilting thread, and a thimble to fit the middle finger of your sewing hand. Most quilters also use a frame or hoop to support their work.

1. Thread a needle with a single strand of quilting thread, knot one end, and insert the needle in the top layer about 1" from the place where you want to start stitching. Pull the needle out at the point where quilting will begin and gently pull the thread until the knot pops through the fabric and into the batting.

2. Take small, evenly spaced stitches through all three quilt layers. Place your other hand under the quilt so that you can feel the needle point with the tip of your finger when a stitch is taken and then rock the needle up and down through all layers until you have three or four stitches on the needle. Pull the thread through so it lies evenly on the fabric, being careful not to pull too tight.

3. To end a line of quilting, make a small knot close to the last stitch; then backstitch, running the thread a needle's length through the batting. Gently pull the thread until the knot pops into the batting; clip the thread at the quilt's surface.

Machine Quilting

For straight-line quilting, it's extremely helpful to have a walking foot to help feed the quilt layers through the machine without shifting or puckering. Some machines have a built-in walking foot; other machines require a separate attachment. Read the machine's instruction manual for special tension settings to sew through extra fabric thicknesses.

For curved designs or stippling, use a darning foot and lower the feed dogs for free-motion quilting. Free-motion quilting allows the fabric to move freely under the foot of the sewing machine. Because the feed dogs are lowered, the stitch length is determined by the speed at which you run the machine and feed the fabric under the foot. Practice on scraps until you get the feel of controlling the motion of the fabric with your hands.

Binding

The quilt instructions tell you how wide to cut the strips for binding. Bindings are generally cut anywhere from 2" to 2½" wide, depending on personal preference. You'll need enough strips to go around the perimeter of the quilt plus 12".

1. Sew the strips together end to end to make one long piece of binding. Join the strips at right angles and stitch from corner to corner. Trim the excess fabric and press the seam allowances open.

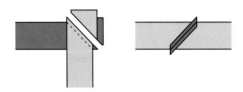

2. Trim one end of the binding strip at a 45° angle. Turn under ¼" and press.
3. Fold the strip in half lengthwise, wrong sides together, and press.

Fold line

4. Trim the batting and backing even with the edges of the quilt top.
5. Starting in the middle of one side and using a ¼"-wide seam allowance, stitch the binding to the quilt. Keep the raw edges even with the quilt-top edge. Begin stitching 1" to 2" from the start of the binding. End the stitching ¼" from the corner of the quilt and backstitch. Clip the threads.

6. Turn the quilt so that you'll be stitching along the next side. Fold the binding up, away from the quilt; then fold it back down onto itself, even with the raw edge of the quilt top.

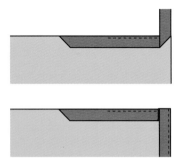

7. Stitch from the fold of the binding along the second edge of the quilt top, stopping ¼" from the corner as before. Repeat the stitching and mitering process on the remaining edges and corners.
8. When you reach the starting point, cut the end 1" longer than needed and tuck the end inside the beginning. Stitch the rest of the binding.

9. Fold the binding over the raw edges of the quilt to the back and blindstitch in place.